The author was born in Dublin and at the age of seven his parents moved to West London where he grew up. At 17 he joined the navy and travelled across the five oceans of the world. Michael has written three books. In 2005 he retired to Spain.

Dedication

This book is dedicated to the memory of my late father, Dano O'Mahony, and my mother, Mary.

Their merit deserves reward for all the hard years they had to endure, and to all the tenants who lived in 29, Fairholme Road, because they made this book possible.

They, along with my parents, went through the performance of living their lives in 29, Fairholme Road. The performance was life itself. To the living I say thank you. To the dead I say may you rest in peace. My Fairholme days will remain with me forever.

Michael O'Mahony

MY FAIRHOLME ROAD DAYS

AUSTIN MACAULEY
PUBLISHERS LTD.

ISBN 978 184963 812 8

www.austinmacauley.com

First Published (2014)
Austin Macauley Publishers Ltd.
25 Canada Square
Canary Wharf
London
E14 5LB

Printed and bound in Great Britain

Foreword

This book is based on my life. The setting is 29, Fairholme Road, West Kensington, London W14.

To ask what it is about, it is all about living in a lodging house, from a landlord's son's point of view. There are many bad landlords but this is a true story of one of the few good ones, who lived in a house and street for thirty-five years. It's about real characters from all walks of life, who came through our front door. To read this book you need a sense of humour. It is sensitive at times so it is not for the soft hearted; it is all about the hard facts of life for the people who had to live in that house and street. It is all true; there is no fiction in this book.

It tells of my childhood and early manhood, days when I lived in that house, I did not live like a normal child; I was the son of a private landlord yet I lived in a house where privacy was limited to four walls. I learnt about life and people from a very early age. At times it was difficult. To my father, our house was not only a home, it was a business first and foremost, and I learnt all the ups and downs as my life was part of it.

Shakespeare said that the world is a stage; well 29, Fairholme Road was a stage and we had some characteristic actors come and go in some of the scenes in our house and street. It was a stage of life.

If you want to find out more just turn the pages.

Chapter One

The Street, the Abbey and the Boat

My days, my Fairholme Road days, in London some thirty-five years ago.

It all started first, though, in Ireland. I was born in the Rotunda Hospital in Dublin. I was brought up in a small little cafe-cum-bed and breakfast-cum-boarding-house-cum-one night stop for people going to and from other parts of Ireland.

We moved some six years later – I do not know why we had to leave in a hurry. I was brought up in Pearse Street, named after one of our Irish heroes. Part of the street was pulled down to make way for modernisation and a fast route straight through to Dublin Airport. At the time I was brought up in it, it was a street. It had a lot of history, voices from the past like Oscar Wilde and the Abbey Theatre. As a child, I played around those famous spots on a three wheel bicycle. That caused more trouble than I care to remember.

We had to get out of Dublin quick because things were changing fast. The airport was getting bigger and people were starting to come into Dublin by plane more frequently; before they used the old mail boat out to Dun Laoghaire.

We left on a bright summer's evening in September 1953. If I remember, my father, with the help of the Dublin police, left Dublin pretty sharply. He was a publican-cum-auctioneer-cum-small business man. We left Dublin on a Friday evening. I remember vaguely, as a child everything looked so big to me. Everything does when you're small and so young. I went up the gangplank at seven in the evening, amid the hustle and bustle of thousands of other people making the same trip. I was making it for the first time; others made it on several occasions, some after seeing their relations, some maybe in sadness, returning to England after burying somebody, a thing that makes the Irish people return home.

I was a little Dublin jackeen who knew no other world. My whole world changed and collapsed around me and my three wheeled bike. My father had a fight over it outside Townsend Street with another gentleman, who is most probably dead and gone and has left this world by now.

When we left Dublin, the only thing I could remember about the trip over is that everyone kept saying on the ship that the name of the ship was *The Hibernian*. I don't know much about *The Hibernian*, only to me it stunk – the smell of drink, sweat and sickness. People got sick, huddled together. Some call it the B & I cattle boat days; those days were far different from today. It was a long journey, taking six hours before we arrived in Holyhead, which was only halfway to London, My mother had with her, her only possession – one trunk carrying the few things she had from her home. We made our way onto the London train, tired and weary after passing through customs. They just laughed at our bits and pieces.

It was a terrible trip for a child, a terrible trip even for an adult for the first time. In those days people had not got a clue where they were going to. We arrived at London Euston about seven o'clock the following morning, very tired and weary.

Chapter Two

Big City in the Eyes of a Child

If I remember rightly, my mum, my dad and me – I was an only child – we made our way to Victoria, It all looked massive to me, London with its big streets, its big lights. I had never seen so many people coming and going in different directions; it was quite frightening.

We arrived at this address my father had. I will always remember that house because, when we went in the door, all I could see in the passageway were vases and vases full of marbles. This woman had stacks of marbles and I was fascinated by them. That night we slept three of us in one little room, me on a shabby little made-up mattress. I remember this lady saying to my dad, "You are very lucky you know; people won't take children. Not in London," she stressed in a nasty manner, "not in guest houses or boarding houses." We stayed there for three days roughing it until we finally split up.

My mum went to the Osterley Hotel down by Hounslow way; she got a job working in the cloakroom. There were not many trades the Irish had only navvying, or the bar game – my father knew all about the bar game, but that is another story. After looking around for days, my dad got a job as a barman in London, around the Elephant and Castle. We walked along the streets – how they looked completely massive and strange. For the first three or four days I could not understand the way these people spoke. Now I speak the same way as them.

My mother took me to stay with her for a few days in the hotel where she worked; she asked the governor and he said I could stay with her. My parents settled down to work. They then decided, or somebody decided, that it would be a good idea to stick me into a boarding school down in Cuffley, Hertfordshire. My dad had a few bob saved up after selling the place in Ireland. He then made up his mind and told my mother that she could no longer keep me with her as he was living in and she was living in, so there was no room for me, so they stuck me in a boarding school which was run by nuns. I hated every minute of it, except for one time when we had a French teacher, who started to try to teach me to play the piano. As a child, I was very slow and backward. I don't know why – it must have been on my mother's side, as my father was a well-educated man. I know, for an Irishman, he could read, write and spell brilliantly, compared with some people today. He had the three Rs, reading, writing and arithmetic, and three months' commercial college. He was quite a brainy man.

I was put down in Hertfordshire with these kids who were in a worse state than I was. Some of them had no proper clothing. When I went down there, they told my father that I had to have all my own clothes, marked up with my name on them. My dad went out and bought everything, even down to the eiderdown. After two or three weeks, the nuns took the clothes off my back, and put them on the other kids. My dad paid a massive bloody fee. I do not know what it was, but it was a lot of money.

After about eleven months in this place, the nuns were starving us out – porridge and boiled eggs in the winter, morning, noon and night. In the summer we ate like rabbits – lettuce, lettuce and more lettuce at lunchtime; for supper we had cheese and potatoes. How I hated cheese and potatoes! After about twelve months, some other kids and I decided we had had enough, so we decided to break out and make a run for it. It was not easy. We had one nun, Sister Ambrose her name was – she was a hard lady; she used to take your trousers down if you got out of hand. I got caught once. In the dormitory this kid in the next bed to me was always crying – mind you, we all did a fair share of that – but this kid never stopped crying. One evening we got fed up with him. We did not know what he was crying for, some of the time. He used to piss the bed. This evening he went one better – he got so frightened, he was looking for it all round the bed. Sister Ambrose heard the racket and came into the dormitory. I, like an idiot, got out of bed and tried to help him out in some way or another. She cornered me, caught me and marched me downstairs. Down with my trousers and her slipper right across my bare backside! It was not very pleasant – some of those nuns had big feet!

When they had put us to bed in the dormitory the next evening and had gone to bed themselves, we started acting out our own Colditz story. We tied a couple of sheets to the bed and climbed out of the window. The only trouble was that the sheets were not long enough to go all the way down, so we had to jump. There were three of us in all. I fell over – I don't know what I fell into nettles or whatever rubbish was behind the back of the dormitory. My legs were grazed but I got up. It would not have worried me if they had split right open; I had only one thing in my head, and that was to get away from that place. We scampered as quickly as we could. The only silly thing was that we had our blazers on, which had our school badge and name written all over it. When we got down to the station we went in and saw the ticket man; he asked us where we were going at that time of night. We said, to London. He said to us that the next train to London was not for another hour. We had just missed one to King's Cross, so we would have to wait for the next one. He got suspicious and got on the bloody phone to the convent, who by that time must have got wind that we were making a dash for it. When we realised what was happening, we ran up to the end of the platform. I kept running along the track: I did not know where I was going, I just kept running and running. The other two kids were running alongside of me – one other bloke made it besides me; the other one either gave up or got caught. I do not know what happened to him.

We saw this train approaching us; it was an old shunter goods train. I will never forget the noise, it was terrifying. It had eight or nine wagons on it, and we thought maybe we could get into one of them, but the driver stopped on purpose to ask us what the bloody hell we were doing on the track, and did we know we were breaking the law and ninety-nine other things. I asked him where he was going. He said, "Never you mind where I am going, I will get the police on to you."

I said, "Listen. Mister, are you going towards London?"

Then he looked at his mate the fireman. I think they looked at us with pity in their eyes. I think they thought we had a lot of spunk in us to go out on that track at that time of night. He said to me, "We are going as far as Watford."

That was well out of the way from where we were going, but he told us he would take us to the next station, which he did. I cannot remember the name of the station; we just went in and waited there. We had no tickets or anything. We got in the last carriage but one, when the train came in. I heard the guard shouting, "Ten fifteen to King's Cross." I knew my mum and dad came from King's Cross when they came down to see me on previous occasions. How I had longed for them to come down and see me on Sundays, with my pocket money – half a crown, which the nuns sometimes nicked off me. By Christ, those nuns had a lot to answer for! We got on the train and when we got to King's Cross, the journey seemed to have taken forever. It must have been about twelve o'clock at night.

When we got off the train, there were all these little carts going by, so we jumped on the back of one of them, and we stuck our heads under the canvas. I think they were post office bags. We jumped off again when we saw there was no one manning the ticket barriers. I think maybe they thought all the passengers had disembarked and that the train was empty so they just went away. When we were clear, we went downstairs. The other bloke said to me, "I know where I am going; do you know where you are going?"

All I had was a bit of paper, with the name and address of the hotel where my mother was working at the time. Then I remembered her telling me some time before, that she and my dad had been going to look at houses in West Kensington and at Shepherd's Bush, but could not agree which one to buy.

I did not have much money on me – I think I had about one shilling and sixpence – so I went up to this cab. The taxi driver said, "Where to?"

I said, "I want to go there," and showed him the piece of paper.

He looked at it, and said, "Cor blimey, that's the other side of London, the Osterley Hotel, Hounslow. Are you sure you have got the money to pay for this?"

"Yes," I said, "I have got the money."

I had no money but the one shilling and sixpence.

"I don't know if I should take you," he said. I think he felt sorry for me; he saw me in short trousers and it was a bloody cold night. "Get in, son," he said.

I said, "I just want to get home to my mum, mister."

"Okay," he said.

I got in the cab and off I went.

My mum came out of the hotel, took one look at me and could not believe where I had popped out from and how I got there. She paid the cabby; it cost a lot of money to go across London in those days – twelve and six or fifteen shillings, I can't remember. It was still a lot of money in 1954. She took me into the hotel that night. I was home as far as I was concerned, I was with my mum and I was not going back to the convent ever again.

The next day my father came down. He said, "I am taking him out of there because he is starving, he has been starved."

My mum insisted I would not go back, and kept me with her for a few more days in the Osterley Hotel. Then we made our way down to West Kensington. My parents had looked at this house in Fairholme Road, this great big house that they were going to buy. My father believed he could not afford it. It had sitting tenants in the ground floor and basement; on the top floor was another sitting tenant from the time of the war; the middle floor was empty. In all, there were ten rooms, not including one bathroom and three toilets, two inside the house and one outside. They had thought about it and thought about it. They had been back down to Shepherd's Bush and looked at more property down there. Willmotts had quite a few of them for public auction; it was a great time for buying. The old gentry days in London were over. The gents were moving out, and selling their houses to anyone who would buy them, including local authorities such as local councils. This started in the period at the end of World War Two. Fairholme Road was like a lot of others in London years ago. They were typical of that time; they were gentry houses, which gents used to stay in during the week and go to their country estates at the weekend. They were houses for people who lived in the days of servants. The servants, years ago, lived in the basement. That was in the thirties and forties but it was all over in the fifties.

I stayed in the Osterley Hotel and helped my mother with the coats, giving people tickets. The old saucer was out there and she got two bob or half-crown tips; those were the days when people gave you tips. She did quite well out of it.

By this time, my parents had stopped arguing about whether to buy the house in Fairholme Road or the house in the Bush and had decided which house they were going to buy. The sale was going through and was nearly complete. It was to be the one in Fairholme Road, so my story of 29, Fairholme Road begins in September 1954. I don't know of a lot of children who were brought up in a boarding, lodging or commercial house, or whatever you want to call them. But I had one hell of a life; it was not always good, but it was not always bad. When people say, 'Have you got anything to say about your life?' most people have lives where they go to work and they come home and nothing out of the ordinary happens. But Fairholme Road was different. Fairholme Road was an unusual story, a nightmare at times, at other times a great pleasure. It was all about life and people.

I am going to tell you about those people and that house. I did not go back to the boarding school in Cuffley anymore.

Chapter Three

My Childhood Fairholme Days: A Kid Full of Fight

My father bought 29, Fairholme Road in September 1954 for the sum of one thousand one hundred pounds from a Mr Dixon who was a solicitor in Earl's Court Road. He sold it to him on a mortgage system; my father paid a small deposit, I do not know how much. He then paid a fixed amount into the bank each month.

Mr Dixon advised my father that when he had paid for the house, not to put the deeds in a local bank. I do not know why, but at that time people did not trust local banks in London. He also told my father to deal with a bank, up in the Strand, which my father did. That bank was William and Glenn. That is where the deeds were deposited some twenty years later, when the house was paid for. My father had money coming from Ireland, from the house that he had sold over there. I do not think he ever got all of it.

To continue with the first stages of 29, Fairholme Road, when we moved into the house, we only had the middle room upstairs. In the top flat was a gentleman called Mr Harvey; he was the last of the old gents. On the ground floor was a London lady, who was of Greek extraction, with two beautiful daughters. There were two Yanks after the girls, who ended up marrying them.

The Yanks were still quite popular around London at that time; there were still a few of them who stayed on after the war. Some of them were based around the outskirts of London. Croydon and places like that, with quite a few Canadians as well.

Back to Fairholme Road. Mrs Papameturia had the ground floor flat. She was subletting the basement to a Mr and Mrs Neville, who had a family of four or five children. She used to get a small amount of money from them.

The first thing my parents did as soon as we moved into the house was to get me fixed up with a school. The new school I went to was called St Thomas More, which was the local Catholic school in Fulham. I then started to get to know some of the people who lived in the street. We had one room, and three of us had to live in it. There was one other room, which my father later found out to be vacant; he did not know about it at first because he never had the keys to it. It was the first room he ever let, to a young guy. At that time he charged something around a pound a week.

I settled down and went to school. For about six to eight months afterwards, my mother worked at the same place and my dad was working away. He was paying so much every month to Mr Dixon for the house. I do not think it was a large amount but, as I said, the banks dealt with it in those days. Building societies were not around; they did not arrive in London until around 1965.

My new way of life started in a strange city. At the school I went to I started to mix in with the other kids; there were kids from my own local area and there were other kids like me who came over from Ireland. I was beginning to mix with all nationalities, also with a lot of other people who came to this country after the war and settled here. Most of them were Irish, Poles, and Scots.

I started to meet some of the families that lived down the street. There were two prefabs at the end of the street; there were houses there originally. During the Second World War I heard that they were hit by bombs, and that some people were killed. I am not too sure, but I think the man who lived in the top flat in our house, Mr Harvey, had lost his sister in the basement of one of the houses when it got bombed.

The houses, like I said, were replaced by two prefabs. In one of the prefabs were a family called the Coles. They were English people born and bred. I think they had two or three daughters, if I can remember. Then there were the Silverstones; there was Milly who was a Scottish lady who liked a drink. Mr Silverstone worked for British Railways. He was a little Scottish Jewish man. I soon found out that not all

Jewish people are rich. A lot of people think all Jewish people are rich. Take it from me that a lot of them are poor. Mr Silverstone went and worked for British Rail, on the Scotland run from Euston to Inverness or somewhere in Scotland. He had a tough time bringing up five kids; it was not easy. They were not bad kids.

There was another family, the Allens. They were Polish and as rough as hell. The Ryans were Irish. They had two girls and, like us, were Catholics. There was one more family, called the Pollards. They were of Polish descent, so we had a good mixture in the street, English, Poles, Scots and Irish. As for the house, after about eighteen months, Mr Harvey announced to my father that he was leaving; his mother had died and left him a cottage down in Cornwall. My dad thought he would want some money or something, but, no, he just up and left, and gave my father the keys: so he then had the top flat and the middle. It was some time before he was going to get the ground floor and the basement. I will tell you about that as we progress.

In the meantime, I was having a bit of trouble at school. I do not know why I was not settling down too well, but I was always getting into fights. I was very small for my age; I never grew properly due to meningitis. As a youngster I was very small and frail. I was fed up with people bullying me. Maybe it was the Irish in me, I do not know, but I just would not take people bullying me. A lot of kids did, they had to take it, but not me. It did not matter how big they were, if they came at me, they found out they were not going to kick the shit out of me and get away with it. This little guy stood up and defended himself. I had a crazy reputation, I do not know why I got it so young, but I saw a kid in the playground fighting another kid, and the smaller kid did to the bigger one exactly what I started to do afterwards. I copied him. He never stopped hitting the bigger one, until he pressed him completely into submission, until he cried out. Unfortunately, I got a reputation for it; I was starting to take on kids not meaning to; it just happened overnight.

I went to school, and had rows and fights. The trouble was I hit back and I hit viciously. Though I was only small I and thin, I was wiry. People said I had a strong punch, though I did not know it. One evening, the headmaster, kept me in the classroom. I got a little bit upset about it, because I thought it was not my fault. The next day I got I involved again. We were all messing around; unfortunately for me, I was the one who got caught. The headmaster got hold of me by my ears. I do not like anyone pulling my ears. My mother would give me beatings across the legs and the backside that I was used to, but I was not used to anyone pulling my ears, or hitting me on the head, not until I came to London. Then I found out that that was the procedure in schools here at that time. The headmaster paid the price for holding onto my ears. I picked up a chair, and hit him around the back of the head with it. The next thing I know is my father, who never interfered and who left my mother to deal with me, got a letter from my school, saying, 'your son Michael O'Mahony is no longer required at St Thomas More school, and should be sent to a special school in Hammersmith, where they will be able to cater for him.'

I was then approaching the age of eleven. I never took the eleven plus as they said I was too backward to take it. They never bothered with me, they just got me out of St Thomas's pretty sharply and sent me down to Hammersmith to a school called St Huberts. There I met some of the roughest kids and the toughest characters in West London. At that time it was nearly all white kids. That was halfway through the year of 1957. In September 1957, the special school I went to transferred to East Acton.

In the meantime, my father was letting the rooms in the house to more lodgers. They were nothing out the ordinary; they were just working men who went to work, paid the rent and caused no problems.

Chapter Four

The Black Man, 1957 to 1965

In late August of 1957, everything changed in the street for the first time. A new nationality of people were coming in who were going to change the whole way of our life, and the ordinary way of English people's lives.

We had settled down to the Londoner's way of life – from bed to work, that was the way life was. That was how my parents earned a living. My father survived slowly, trying to save every penny to make ends meet and pay so much down on the house every month.

Then came the black man. I had never seen a black man until I came to London. August 1957 was the first time my eyes saw one. That month my father caused uproar with the white people we had staying in the house for a short time. This was no good for my father's business, so he thought of a great idea. The black men had nowhere to live; a lot of them had their wives, some had girlfriends they met on the boat on the way over – yes they called them their women. It seems funny thirty years later; we have adapted to their way of life. Back in 1957, they had started living in sin as far as the church and the state were concerned. They came in their droves, not only to Brixton but to all parts of London. They came to West Kensington. My dad was the first white man to take them in the door, he saw them as foreigners like himself; they had nowhere to live so he gave them a room, and they paid him thirty bob for a single and three pounds for a double room. It caused hell and havoc; the hatred and jealousy started with the white people. I must admit, it did not please my mother at first either, she found it hard for three of us to live in one room. This was only the beginning; we moved up to the top landing and took the front room. The gas cooker was on a space on the top landing. My father took in Mr and Mrs Cato on the same landing and they shared the cooker with us. I believe they were married; Mrs Cato was a Catholic. She was a nice woman. She had a lot of trouble and aggro with her husband. Mrs Cato and my mother got into some terrible tights, shocking fights – an Irish woman and a black woman, you can imagine, no holds barred. She used to give my mum a terrible hiding but my mum would not lie down; she kept coming back for more. My dad tried to keep the two women apart but it was not easy.

That was the first bit of tension. My father then let off the middle floor to two more black people. The blacks worked hard; a lot of them had trades: they had good trades. Some were carpenters, welders, fitters, and. yes, a lot of them did work on London Transport. We took in, on the middle floor, Mr Blanche and Marge Springer. They were never married in those days – that was criminal. My dad never worried as long as they were no trouble. They paid my dad the rent every week – tell a lie, it was me! I must have been the youngest little landlord in town. I was eleven years old and I used to collect the rent around the house on a Friday at seven p.m. I was finished at twenty past seven. They were tremendous people to pay the rent in those days; they could not go into the pubs because they could not get served by the landlords because of the trouble it would cause. I used to go into the off-licence, and buy them a bottle of VP Red Biddy wine at three and six. They used to send me out on small errands for fags, ten Waites or Woodbines. They gave me sixpence for going – I could never get enough. They stayed indoors at weekends and ate chicken. The womenfolk sang and, by Christ, did they like washing! They used to wash their clothes up in the bathroom non-stop. All over the weekend, the bathroom was going like the clappers. They were big women, some hard-looking, some fine-looking too. They used to call my mum and dad Master and Mistress Mahoney.

Getting back to the white population in the street, we became public enemy number one with them because we took these black people in. How they hated us! The kids started to take the piss out of me in the street with all the aggro and started saying we had our own monkeys. We have this now and all the racism and the rest of it; the only difference was that the kids in the street soon found out that I was not going to be laughed or sneered at. I could not run as well as the English kids and London kids but, by Christ, when I caught them. I gave them fucking hell. I gave them such a hiding that they did not forget it. After a couple of years in the street, the kids started to have a bit of respect for me; in the meantime, the black and white thing got worse and we had fights out in the road with both black and white people. My dad did not bother anybody: he stayed clear of everybody. He walked up and down the street; the trouble was that none of them had the guts to come near him to say anything about what he had in the house because he was not exactly a small man. We had ding-dongs of trouble because we had black men going out with white women. That started a lot of trouble. They were also trying to get served in the pubs.

When I was about twelve or thirteen, I was knocking about with a young white girl, a London girl. Then, believe it or not, she took a fancy to a black fellow. It seems funny now but I got really jealous at the time. I did not know where to put my face but I grew out of it. I learnt how to live with them and how to work with them. I respected them too as time went by; as years passed we all learnt to put up with each other as we had to. That was the street I lived in.

Now, some more characters. Take this guy, for instance, Kevin Sullivan and myself. We were punching shit out of each other for some years before his father came up to my father and informed him that we were related as first cousins.

The blacks did their thing in their own way. Boy did they like parties as well! They used to say to my dad that they were getting married, or any excuse for a party. When they had a wedding it went on for three or four days but my dad never took a blind bit of notice because my dad liked a drink himself. They always used to bring him up a bottle of white rum. It was white rum, the real McCoy from their homes, like Trinidad, Jamaica and Barbados, the Islands those people came from. It was not easy for them. We knew how they felt when they first arrived in this country because we had the same problem. At first they did not arrive with many children but as the years went by, they did. The ones we had were just young couples and single guys; the kids came later. We had two or three born in 29, Fairholme Road.

My days as a kid were amusing. I think I grew up pretty fast. Sometimes I wanted to stay behind. Like all kids, we had a gang down our street. We had a leader whose name was Watson, who later emigrated to Canada; he was quite a character. He took us down to the old Empress Hall; we broke into it and stole the keys that opened all the doors in the building. We got the keys that led to the old Coalwharf building, broke in there and stole two thousand cigarettes plus sweets. We scarpered off with the keys that were no good to us. Somebody must have been doing their nut. The police, or the Old Bill as we used to call them, soon got the wind of it; they came looking for us. We had to climb a twenty foot advertising board to get back down under to the level of the pavement. This was at the back of buildings alongside Depee Street. It's all gone now, replaced with high council flats. At that time, going down Northend Road, West Kensington, there were law cars going up and down the road like the clappers. Just as I got around the corner, there was a police van – or, as we used to call them, a meat wagon, a Black Maria to those who remember them. Inside were all my mates and I swore blind that I did not know anyone of them. My first big lie! When the policeman said to me, "Do you know any of this lot? Are you associated with them? Have you been over that Coalwharf?"

I said, looking up to him, with a high voice, "No, no, Officer, not me, my mum would not let me associate with them kind of people. She told me to keep away from them." I was lucky that he fell for it. The tears ran down my small face, end of act one! The kids in the meat wagon just looked on with open mouths. I had conned the copper and them! I was always getting a belting across the legs from my mother; she thought the kids in the street were a bad influence on me. Little did she realise I was influencing the kids! Anyway, Mr Watson and our little gang used to do weird things like stealing cigarettes out of shops and all the things that kids did. We used to get up to capers. We were not always bad. We used to go along to the parties that were going on with the black people in the street; they used to go on for days.

Number 19, Fairholme Road was a right old knocking shop to some, or should I say whorehouse or house of immoral earnings, whichever way you want to put it. There were six or seven white girls working in it. Nearly all the customers were black; quite a few of the guys who were staying in our place were going in and out of it. We used to get the beer bottles that used to come out of there; we used to scrounge them by going down in the basement. We used to get fourpence, old money, by taking them back to the off-licence. The man in the off-licence used to wonder where we got all the beer bottles from but I used to tell him they were from our house. Some of them did come from our house but not all of them. One day, we went back there and the off-licence bloke got all uptight and annoyed, and he said to me. "I am not serving you anymore. You are taking all that beer and wine back to those blacks in your house and all the houses down there."

I said to him, "I do not give a monkey's if you serve me or not, I will take the bottles somewhere else." I used to take them to the pubs sometimes, but the pubs would not always take them if they did not have their mark on them. I used to hop the wag – what's known as truancy. I got fed up with school; I learnt nothing. It was my fault; I was wrong. The last two years of my schooling were the best years of my schooldays, as our teacher let us learn the subjects that we liked. At last we got to be treated as young men, not hard case kids. I got a thirst for history and general knowledge and did very well. My father did not like the way I was not getting it right at school so he made me stay on another year. If my father knew that I skipped school he would have been very upset with me. He never laid a hand on me; he used to leave that to my mother. I knew that if he hit me I would not get up for a week. He only had to give me one of his hard looks and that scared the shit out of me. My mother used to cover up for me sometimes; she would give me a sick note when I was not sick.

As a young boy of twelve, I did not know much about girls. My first experience was down in my father's coal cellar. I went along with three other young boys who had a young girl of the same age. We took turns at her. Until then I did not know that it was for more than just peeing with. We were smoking the fags that we had stolen from the Coalwharf in the cellar at the same time as shagging a twelve year old girl. We took packets of Omo and Daz washing powder down the cellar. This was a crazy idea that the guy who lived next door to me had. He got a bucket and filled it up with water and the two full packets of washing powder. Standing the girls up against the wall naked, he then soaked his penis in the soapy water and put it between the young girls' legs.

Not only did we have smoke from the fags going up through the manhole covers from the coal cellar, we had soap and bubbles too. We did not know what the hell we were doing but it was something different and we tried it.

But, getting back to what we thought was more exciting at the time, was when the police came into the house one evening looking for a few of the kids and this bloke Watson who had nicked the goods from the Coalwharf. All the time, I had them hiding in the basement which the coppers were standing over, and they did not know it was there. The police searched the whole street and our house; they never found them that night. The place came in handy for hiding goods. Some years later, my father discovered the place: luckily for me, it was empty at the time. He never said anything to anyone, only had the floor filled in. We used to ransack empty houses and steal from them. We were forever stealing.

Going back to the house, some of the capers and things that were happening there were quite incredible. The black people started to fight amongst themselves; they fought over their women; sometimes their women would get involved with other men. It used to cause big trouble. We had Mr Cato upstairs in the top flat. He decided to go across the road to 26, where there was a prostitute offering her services. She was an

Irish girl who was a cracking bit of stuff whom he used to go to; she did not care who her customers were as long as the money was there. Mrs Cato one night went mad, put on my dad's hat, got into a raging temper and went across the road looking for this woman. On that occasion she did not find her, she came back and when she found her husband in, she said to him, "Don't come near me. You are diseased or you could be diseased."

As time went on, the house started to change. My father never had the whole house; he only had the top and middle floors. Mrs Papameturia, who was of Greek descent, had control of the ground floor and the basement. She was a sitting tenant since the war. My father bought the house with her in it. He got an income of one pound seven and six a week. She was at that time known as a controlled tenant. Mrs Papameturia had a problem with her two daughters downstairs. She wanted to get them married to two Yankee sailors. At this time, my dad knew of the problem and thought it would be a good time to do a bit of business and put a proposal to her that he would give her seven hundred pounds to get out. He said to her that she could get herself a council place and she could get her daughters married off and he would get it drawn up by a solicitor to make it all legal. Well, she did not want to know at first. She asked him to make it a thousand pounds; he told her straight that he had not got that much.

As time went on, the girls started to give her a hard time; they wanted the fellows and they wanted to get out of London. And they knew there was a better life in the States for them so one evening she had had enough and she approached my dad. She said she would take him up on the deal so my dad got a bottle of whisky and a couple of glasses and he went down and got his solicitor. They then drew up a deal that she would vacate the ground floor and authorise the people downstairs in the basement, who she was subletting to, to leave for the agreed price of seven hundred pounds, so it was agreed in good will. My father said he would throw in a wedding party and he did just that. He threw a party for them and the Yanks loved it. The daughters got the Yanks and the Yanks got the money, then everybody had a good time all round. Mrs Papameturia and the Nevilles left downstairs and the basement, and for the first time since my dad moved into the house twelve years before, he had control of the whole house.

He then let the ground floor to two more West Indian couples, Mr Albert and his woman and a young coloured girl. I forget her name but she used to bring a fellow in and you could always tell if she was at it because she had a certain way of sitting on the bed. How I used to know is, when I used to go in the room to collect the rent from them all on a Friday evening, I used to give them all one pair of sheets and two pairs of pillowcases and I would sign their books on my dad's behalf. I would collect three pounds for a double room and one pound ten shillings, old money, for a single room.

My dad was up the pub one day and he met these two old characters. One was called Dick and the other one was called Mac MacCarthy. Dick was a Londoner, who had served in everybody's army; he had been in the Foreign Legion, the British Army and even been in the Free State Army back in Ireland. He was quite a character and had seen a lot of life. He was going to see some more life when he came to 29, Fairholme Road.

Mac MacCarthy was a northerner of Irish parents. He had money years ago but like a lot of men he fell on hard times. The problem was the drink. It was a problem for a lot of people who lived in Fairholme Road and 29 had a lot of alcoholics. I don't mean to be disrespectful as I loved my parents very much, yet I have to say that they both had a bad alcohol problem. If anyone lived in that house they would have had some problem. Alcohol, or drink as we called it, was a way out for a short time. Like all drugs, it took the worries away until you woke up drowsy in the real world again, full of temper and sick. All the people that lived in number 29 had a hell of a lot to put up with. When my parents hit the bottle hard, shouting and fighting like mad dogs. They slagged each other off right, left and centre and myself and all the house got the full blast.

Never a night went by when someone did not lose their keys. You had to go down and let them in as we lived on the premises. When you opened the door, if they were drunk you sometimes got a nasty mouthful. Sometimes you had to put them to bed. I learnt never to upset a drunk, just listen and put up with all they said. If they said green was red, that was all right by me! At one in the morning sometimes the drunk would start a row with his woman. If it got out of hand you would have to go and stop it. One thing we did not lack was excitement. We had an exhibition every weekend – it was some lodging house!

Getting back to Dick and Mac, they moved into the end room in the basement. It was incredible that two such big men could fit into such a small room with two small beds, a wardrobe, a sink, a table and an old paraffin heater. Mac was over six feet two inches in height. My dad charged them thirty bob each. Next to them was a West Indian couple. She was a gorgeous young girl about nineteen or twenty – she could not have been any more than that. She was living with a fellow who was a carpenter. He was not a bad bloke. Then in the front room of the basement was another West Indian couple with a young child. Their names were Mr and Mrs Bristol. Mrs Bristol was always going around half naked, she thought sometimes she was God's gift to men, and even with young boys like myself she used to try it on. She tried it on with me but my father told me one thing – never mix business with pleasure, not on your own doorstep. Believe it or not, it was tempting at times. I kept my place, though she offered it to me on a plate many times. I did not touch her. There were times when I used to collect the rent: she would be there, wrapped up in a sheet halfway down her. She did not care tuppence. It was boredom that caused her to carry on that way, as the men used to leave the women and go upstairs and play cards. Besides that they were not a bad couple.

So Dick and MacCarthy, the only white men in the basement, were surrounded by West Indians in the jungle, as they said. They felt as if they were the only two white men in the house, and besides my dad, they were, as all the rest were, black people. Dick and MacCarthy could not stand them but my dad did because he needed the money and he was used to them. Anyway, not only could Dick and MacCarthy not stand them but the people next door, who were Londoners, could not stand them either.

We had an Esso man who drove a big Esso motor and he thought he was quite something. He used to bring his motor down the road, jack it up, and was always messing about with it – excuse my expression – flicking about with it when there was no need to. I don't know why English people mess around with cars when there is no need to. They are always out there doing something with the motors when they don't need anything doing to them but this was typical.

The bloke upstairs to him was a bloke called Webb and I knew his son Bobby. He was all right and Mrs Webb was a lovely woman – she came from Oxford. But old man Webb was a right bastard. We had a cat in the house my dad used to keep it for mice and she had kittens, about eight or nine of them. They got out on the back roof: they were flat roofs with a small, low wall between each roof of each house. One day, old man Webb got hold of the kittens and poisoned them, one after another. My mother never forgot it and I didn't either but one boy across the road in the street was outraged over it. This lad was one of the Silverstones, Freddie Silverstone. Freddie was a nice kid. He used to come over to us; it was funny in those days, you could leave your doors open. The front door of our house was always open. The kids used to come and sit on the doorstep and we would talk and play and spin yarns to each other. But the Silverstones were more than that. I used to go to their house and I used to sleep there and they used to sleep in mine when we had a room empty. They used to sleep all in the same bed, believe it or not, three or four fellows – and think nothing of it. We were always fighting with each other, but this day Freddie got very upset about the kittens because I had given him one of the kittens. He had got a stack of plates; I don't know where he got them from. He was younger than me. I was about twelve or thirteen at the time and I think he was about eleven. He crowned Old Man Webb with every plate. It was incredible – an eleven year old boy! He was so strong that he hit a full grown man and he belted hell out of him with all the plates. He let him have them one at a time. Old Man Webb had to go up to the hospital. Afterwards he changed his attitude!

When my dad used to mind his own business and go in after a few drinks, they used to try and take the piss out of him. They would say, "Here comes the nigger-man lover with all those blacks in that house." How we used to get it, one hell of a load of stick! This bloke one day said some nasty kind of remark.

My dad just looked him right in the eye and said, "Excuse me mister, where you're living, is it yours? Do you own it?"

The bloke replied, "Well, I am living in number 27."

"Yes. But do you own it?" asked my dad again. "You have not paid for it."

The bloke did not know where to put his face.

"You're only renting it, aren't you? You're no better than the people in my house." His last words to him were, "The difference between you and me, mister, is I own my house and you don't own yours. You hate my tenants because they are black. You amuse me with your Anglo-Saxon way of thinking. It's amusing. In twenty years from now, London will be half black, you better get used to it."

The bloke got angry and shouted at my dad. "You Irish pig."

My dad just laughed at him. "Why don't you go to the black man's land if you can't stand him over here? My friend, he is here to stay." My father left them standing. He never said any more after that; he just walked up the street to his door. It did not bother him. As the years went by, people got jealous of my father. Up and down Northend Road they took the old man on in fights in pubs. The Coalwharf men had a go at him; they too got jealous of him as they knew he had a few bob. By this time, he was getting to the stage where he had the house nearly paid off. Yes, he had a few bob. He worked by day for a living and he saved his money. They got so jealous of him that they picked a row with him. One thing my old man hated being called was a bastard. They used to call him that; sometimes they used to call him an Irish one and that got his goat up. He hated it so much he used to get stuck into them, and Dano was quite used to fighting and he knew how to fight. That was my dad's name, Dano. He took them on drunk or sober. I think that he only got a hammering once, that was by two Irishmen who got jealous. They beat him up in The Three Kings public house in the toilet, but it took the two of them to do it when he was tanked up one night. But Dano was getting a bit of a reputation now, and so was I. After Watson left the street I became quite a hard man. I would take on anybody, no matter how big they were, the bigger the better.

A guy came into the street one day. His brother was supposed to be the second best fighter in St Edmund's school, which was the biggest school in our neck of the woods. I broke every spoke in his brother's bike. I took him on and beat the shit out of him, then his brother came down and I beat the shit out of him too. There was no one left so then the street was mine, as far as ruling it was concerned. I was the gang leader. As far as my dad was concerned, it did not stop him going out to the pubs on a Friday night but he tried to avoid trouble. He got a reputation for being quite a hard man but he always kept to himself, and eventually it wore off.

If anybody wanted a room, they came to Dano. My dad's worst mistake sometimes was taking people in who he met in public houses. We come now to 1962 and 1964. That was the year I left school. I wanted to be an electrician but it never worked out. They said I would not be strong enough. What a load of rubbish that was! I landed up humping more conduit and heavy gauge conduit and doing heavy lifting than some electricians would ever think of, because in those days they had mates to do all the work and grafting for them. They only did the practical work.

In my dad's house in 1963 some of the black people were starting to pull out. They were starting to get their own places, and good luck to them. The prejudice was slowly going. It took time. It took twenty years for white people to accept that the black people were here to stay. I know there is still some prejudice around today, but the white people had to accept that they were going to work on the buses and the trains and other jobs and their children were starting to grow up in this country, so white people would have to accept them in the future, anyway, because black they may be but they were also English.

By this time my dad had a house half black and half white and, believe it or not, they did get on with each other.

Now I come to the story of another gentleman called Mr Gilmore, who my dad took in out of a pub called the Seven Stars in Northend Road. Mr Gilmore took a room on the middle landing in the back of the house with two other guys named Carney and Cummings, who were professional chemists. They took the front room on the same landing. Cummings had a bad drink habit; he also was a bit of a womaniser. He used and abused and bullied Carney, who was his roommate. Carney was a small, thin man who looked like death warmed up. I don't know why he stayed around Cummings; he must have liked him a lot. He did take some stick from Cummings. Mr Gilmore was in the same boat as far as the drink habit went, but Gilmore had a little bit more coming to him. He stumbled on a fortune by sheer luck. One day he picked up an Irish paper called *The Irish Independent* which my mother used to buy as she liked to keep in contact with home sometimes. By reading the paper to Mr Gilmore, she spotted his name. Somebody had died and left land and money. No one had claimed it as there was no living relations left in Ireland or the USA. So this ad was in the paper. The solicitor was trying to contact someone who could prove they were a real relation of this family. Our Mr Gilmore phoned the solicitor and, unknown to us at first, he informed the solicitor that he could prove his people came from that part of Ireland though he never put one foot in Ireland in his life. He was the long lost only nephew who had a lovely English accent. When he made his maiden voyage to Ireland, Gilmore had no money for the trip. Dano lent it to him on the understanding that when he hit the jackpot then Dano would get his money back. So off went Gilmore to Ireland. After some time of signing his life away to solicitors, he returned with loads of money. Unfortunately for Dano, Mr Gilmore did not return to his premises. Mr Gilmore's new bank manager and part-time landlord, was a gentleman called Peter in The Oak public house. He was the manager there. Peter ran up a slate for Mr Gilmore on the condition that he got so much money back, until he ran out of every penny. Well, he bought himself a scooter and got around and everybody had a great time – the same old carry on. Mr Gilmore became famous overnight; all the bums came out of the woodwork while the drink was flowing. They were all up there and there were parties for everybody. A good time was had by all, until one day the bubble burst and reality hit Mr Gilmore in the face, when he ran out of money and Peter said to him, "Well, Mr Gilmore you owe me so much." Mr Gilmore had no more to give to him as he had paid Dano the last three hundred pounds he had. Peter had conned him like a lot of pub managers do when they go cashing cheques for them.

There was another manager down the road from him. I won't say he conned people but he certainly made some money out of builders because a lot of builders had no banks or did not want to use banks and they used to go to him. He had the Clarence public house; they all went to him. I used the pub myself quite regularly when I got older. We had another builder; his name was Paddy MacCrossen who fell off scaffolding and got fourteen hundred pounds compensation. That was a lot of money in those days. Paddy drank black rum; he was always sweating from the rum. He used to send me out to get him more rum, day and night. Sometimes he used it as a livener, meaning a cure, a follow-up drink after the night before. He lived in a small, partitioned room in the front of the house. He always paid my dad the rent. He was all right; he caused no real trouble. It was a shame, it was terrible, when he could not afford to pay my dad any more. It was six or seven weeks without paying any rent before my dad told him he would have to go. Paddy was not helping himself and he was going downhill fast. He lost his job and the drink got hold of him. Sometimes he used to come back at eleven or twelve at night when the pubs were closed, then you would see Paddy go down the basement steps and curl up in the coal house amongst the dustbins. At that time there was an awful lot of dampness in the walls. My father would go down when he was locking up; he would spot Paddy and say to him, "Come out of there, Paddy."

Paddy would reply, "That's all right, Dano. I like small places."

What I am telling you here is the truth, not lies; this is the way these people lived. This was London, the London I lived in, the place I grew up. Drink was a terrible problem. Drink was a way out, as it is with drugs today. In those days there was plenty of work, in fact it was work, to bed or to the pub. There were not many places to go; picture houses were always too full.

The blacks who left in 1968 were the last to go. Mr Cato went and we got the top flat. Then we were approaching the age when the white terror began. Just before the last black people left, Mr Blanche was downstairs. A young half-caste girl came in to see them with some friends. I just want to tell you this story as these were the last of the black people living in the house then. Mr Blanche used to play bridge with friends of his. Marge, Mr Blanche's other half and him were not hitting it off too well, when along came this young lady. She was a lovely looking girl, very pretty. As soon as Blanche saw her, he had his eyes on her. I don't know if he did have an affair there and then but he said he was going back to the West Indies. The plan that he had backfired; Marge found out the two of them were having an affair and she thought she would do likewise. While he was out she brought in a bloke; Blanche got to find out about it, and we all got to find out about it, because one evening all hell broke out, and there was the sound of someone being murdered. Loud screaming and the sound of pain came howling up the stairs; doors were flung open all over the house; people came running out to see what the noise was about. Normally you never heard a bad sound come out of that room, only laughter. We were numb when we found out that Blanche was beating hell out of Marge. She was not a small woman by any means. Marge had a nice smile, was always jolly-looking. She was stocky and around five six in height; Blanche was five nine, well-built. He nearly killed her. The door was closed from the inside. My father got the spare key, went down and got in and stopped him from finishing poor Marge off. It was alright for Blanche to play around but it was not okay for her to do likewise, the same old story.

Within a week Blanche took off; that was the last time we saw him. My father asked Marge to leave but she did not want to go. Marge worked hard for London Transport. She had to work shift hours. A lot of black people did that in those times; not many white people did. My father told Marge that the room was in Mr Blanche's name in the rent book. She left after my father had to give her a solicitor's letter. I was sad to see her go as I liked her a lot. She always had that happy-go-lucky feeling. I came home one night and she was gone – no goodbyes – who could blame her?

Cato's story was a little bit different. They got a flat over in Wandsworth. Judith Cato was a tall, slim-looking woman who had a big smile that showed a wide set of pure white teeth which would put any dentist out of work. Judith had a habit of wearing tight jeans; they made her look very sexy and she knew it too, though she was very sensitive about white people. As she spent more time living in the house, she did flirt a bit with Mr Blanche. Who could blame her, her old man was doing the dirty behind her back. She had a brother, or brother-in-law, I am not quite sure, who lived in the room with them. He was a tall, good-looking fellow about six foot. We became suspicious that something was going on there. Maybe nothing did happen but the guy was always going in and out. Old Cato was working up in Telfers, the pie factory in Fulham. He worked nights; it was doing his health no good, along with the Old Red Biddy wine that he was drinking and the whores that he was knocking around with. He was poxed up to the eyeballs, yet he kept on working away. Judith suffered a lot; I think she had two miscarriages. When they left, my mother had a clear-out of the room afterwards. I was not there during the day as I was now working. The bed was a right mess; the room was in a terrible state. There was dried blood all over the mattress. Black people in those days were very reluctant to go to hospital.

There were a lot of women in that house who had miscarriages and lost children. Sometimes they did not want them and sometimes they had home-made abortions. It was terrible to think of it in that way – that they knew how to get rid of a child. That was the thing to do. I saw from time to time the women with tears in their eyes after having to do what they did.

Just three years before the Catos left, Judith gave birth to a boy in hospital. His name was Clive. He was the first young boy to start his young life in this house. Clive was four when they left. Then my father moved me out of my small room into the Catos' room. I papered and painted it and did it all up. I papered all the rooms in that house. At first we had decorators who came in and they did it all. Some old guy used to come in with his firm; I used to watch him; I learnt from him. I papered, painted, plastered and learnt to bodge. I learnt quite a lot from other people. We had more cowboys than the USA! One time I painted the landings; that was quite something with a four storey house with a fifty foot landing. It was no joke for a fourteen-year-old boy to go and get indoor scaffolding. That was the sort of thing I had to do – like get up in the middle of the night and put felt across a leaking roof as it was lashing down with rain.

Every Friday evening when I came in from school and from work I had to wash the whole house down. When I was at school my father used to give me five bob for cleaning the place down, providing I did it properly, top to bottom. I washed it all down. We had stairs with lino on them; you had to scrub them with carbolic soap – no Hoovers or carpet in those days! Jeyes fluid was used in the toilets, in the yard, on the steps. Just when you thought you had finished, my father came along and checked out all that you had done and if you had not done the job properly he made you do it again. That was my dad to a tee.

We did not get carpet in the place until 1970. Most of the rooms then had lino. The black people then were mad for furniture; they could not get enough of it. My dad used to go down to Hughes Brothers Ltd and get second-hand furniture that years later became antique. It was destroyed before I left Fairholme Road. I sold what was left so that was the end of the black people era. In 29, they pulled out one after another. Some called back many years later and they thanked my father for giving them a roof over their heads in hard times for their generation. They said they were glad he took them in; he too was glad to get them and he said so. They were the only people who paid us regularly; they never missed a week. Now we come to the white era. I will tell you all about them in 29, Fairholme Road.

Chapter Five

The Swinging Sixties and the Hippies, 1964 to 1969

In March of 1968 we took in a young London couple. Their names were Micky and Margaret. Micky was quite a lad; he came from North London, somewhere around the Islington area. Margaret came from East Acton in West London. Micky loved old motors, the trouble being they were not always his. He loved joyriding plus bike scrambling. He made a lot of money out of it when he was not laid up with broken arms or legs etc. He was not a bad bloke and he came into Fairholme Road like a lot of people – he had a lot of problems. One was he could not hold down a job for long. He did try. He was a guy who loved to be free and loved a bit of action. He was not ready for Mag and the two kids he had. Yet Mag was good for him; she slowed him down to face life and the hard facts of life.

Micky lived in the fast lane, wanted a good laugh and to be happy all the time. He and I had some good times. I took him out to the pubs – two pints and he was happy. He did not drink much; nor did I at first. I will never forget the time Micky had an old banger of a Ford Prefect that broke down right in the middle of the King's Road, Chelsea. There we were in this written-off vehicle, with all the best-dressed people in London looking at two young, greasy kids pushing this old banger up the road. We were lucky there was not a copper in sight!

At that time we became a little clique as another guy joined us. His name was Brett Jones. We were led to believe he was from a rich family back in Wales. He had a lot of money tied up in a trust for him. Brett was getting an allowance as far as we knew I certainly think he was never short of money. He used to hang around with a Scottish girl called Fiona. She was blonde, plump and good looking. She knew Mr Jones was loaded so she put herself about with him.

Around Fairholme then, there was our Oliver. He arrived in 1966, just after Dick and Mac left. I say 'our Oliver' as he was just like one of the family. He did all the work in the house on the electrical side. My father trusted him completely: Oliver was brilliant as far as electrical work or electronics was concerned. He was a qualified electrical engineer, but also had problems with his family: he was a loner, another black sheep from a very wealthy family. Oliver was so good he could put his hand to anything. The one problem was that he was so slow, but whenever he did anything it was spot on. He became the maintenance man at number 29. Oliver rewired the whole house. As I worked at the time for an electrical wholesalers, I got all the materials at a reduced price – no, I did not nick it, as my father had to have receipts with the company's name on it for the taxman. Anyway, my father did not believe in fiddling or thieving; he had no time for that, as he regarded it as a sign of weakness of the mind.

So we became a family at number 29 and we all had our own problems: we all came from different backgrounds and nationalities, but we lived together. We had parties; I had one big party one day. I told my dad a pack of lies; I told him a young lady was coming over from The States and that I had to give a good impression, as it was my boss's daughter and it concerned my job. The truth was I was getting bored with the house. Once the black people left it became quiet. I just wanted to liven it up – and did I! We had a party one night – and I mean one hell of a time was had by all. At the time my dad was working for Watney's brewery so we got the beer at a cheap price – all fourteen barrels of ale. It went on from eight in the evening till seven in the morning. We had people coming into the house from my work and from all over West London. We had Oliver on the door as a bouncer, as he looked the part. He was not only big in size all round, he was big, though he would not hurt a fly. As the night went on I did manage to keep control, except for a few gate crashers and one ransacked room. One tenant had a small amount of money stolen, and the stairs were covered with bodies, sick from too much alcohol. There was also loud rock and roll music. We called it having a good time.

It is sad to say that the nicest little man that we had staying with us at the time was Mr Harry Deller. He was from North London, a small, proud cockney man. We used to talk about football; he supported Tottenham in the fifties. I always called him 'Mr Deller' we used to talk for hours on the landing; it upset me a bit that night when I found out he had been robbed as he had the smallest room in the house. When he spoke, he would stutter all the time. He was so lonely; they were all the same until they came to Fairholme, then they could open up and feel safe with us. I never went into what happened to them on their way through life; we did not ask any questions. Some had left their wives or husbands; some just drifted from place to place. Yet when they landed in 29, Fairholme Road they settled down, opened up and started to talk to each other. They come out onto the landings, looked around, then someone started a conversation. They became acquainted overnight.

At this time my mother became very sick in the head; she started to suffer from schizophrenia. We never knew what caused it – maybe it was the change of life; it could have been the pressure in the house. She caused trouble by picking on the tenants in the house. She became very ill; she was shouting, fighting with people. She got so bad that my dad had to get her into hospital. It took three doctors in those days; it was not easy. You had to go to your GP plus two more doctors from the hospital and bring them out at night. If you were lucky they came right away; if you were not, then you had to suffer with the problem all night and that was hell. With my mother she heard voices in her head; she would turn on you as soon as look at you. It was hard to understand how she changed into a sick monster. Each day got worse until she got treatment. My mother went down to Banstead which was a mental hospital for people who suffered from that complaint. There were thousands like her. Though Banstead was in Surrey it was registered under Chelsea and Kensington Authorities. Me and my dad went down to see my mother many times; sometimes she didn't even know we were there as the drugs made her drowsy and put her into another world. She got so bad one time, my dad had to agree with the doctors that she would have to have electric shock treatment. It was the worst thing he agreed to, in my opinion; it drove her nervous system into a nightmare of reality. Never again did my dad agree to the electric shock treatment when he saw the state of my mother afterwards. After all, she had saved his life on one occasion. He did not want to see her suffer further so whenever she got bad again he agreed to injections and tablets only. She came home and for three months or more would be okay then – bang – her head would go again. That was the general pattern. If she got any alcohol, then that would set her off like a bomb. She would give you all she had – abuse, swearing; the sickest words that are not found in a dictionary came out of her mouth. People talk about schizophrenia and what causes the problem. I know one thing – I saw it in my mother from an early age; my dad and I lived with it. My mother's GP asked me how she was. I said, "Not too bad now, doctor."

She replied, "I am sorry to have to tell you that your mother will not ever be cured of schizophrenia."

In those days it was terrible. She kept you up half the night, just walking around effing and blinding like mad. The booze made it so bad, she just could not handle it, but we all have to have something in life. Some people gamble, others womanise and some take to alcohol and drugs. You take your pick or you live a quiet life.

Getting back to Fairholme Road, the white people we had then were okay; they paid their way and we had no trouble. I was living a double life. No one knew at work about 29, Fairholme Road; they thought I lived in a rented flat. If I told anyone, they would say I was crazy to put up with it all. I lived a double life and I learnt how to lie, but I had to learn well because if you are going to tell lies you must have a good memory and memorise all you say; if you don't you will get found out, and I got found out a few times. Yet no one outside of Fairholme and the people I knew had any idea about my life there. Sometimes, I must admit, it was embarrassing to say I lived in that house and the way we lived, yet it was not always bad. I had great times in that house and Fairholme. After all, it was my street, my home; all my life was wrapped around it. I was too scared to leave it; no matter what my mother's and father's problems were, I loved them. As an only son I was lost without them, no matter what their faults were. We had one great guy who became a good friend of mine. He kept to himself for some time but then he came out of his shell. He did some fine work around 29, Fairholme Road for my dad and me. If you gave him a paintbrush there was no stopping him. His name was Patrick and he was of Irish stock from Galway. Patrick was brought up in Manchester. We got on so well, though he was a good twenty-five years older than me. At times he looked after me. He was the best man at my wedding. I don't know the full story of Patrick. I think at one time he told me that he was married with a couple of kids. I do know when he first came to us he could drink like a fish; he would drink ten to fifteen pints and walk straight out the door, say, "See you tomorrow," hold his head up and say, "do you want anything done?" I know it is nothing to be proud of, yet that was the way Patrick was. He could hold his alcohol until, many years later, he became a full-blown alcoholic. Yet in those early days at 29, Fairholme, he was the most sensible man, alongside my dad, who lived in that house, when they did not hit the bottle. Patrick was ex-army; he had been in the Korean war. He had lived life to the full; he kept it bottled up. Patrick and I used to go up to The Elm public house. It became one of our haunts in Northend Road. Sometimes, all the lads who lived in 29, Fairholme used to get together and go out for a few pints. Patrick did not like them going to his drinking hole as he too lived a double life. He did not want anyone who knew him to find out that he lived in 29, Fairholme; it embarrassed him. He told me so. It was not the house; it was some of the people he did not like, yet it was a hiding place as well as a home to lots of blokes just like Patrick. Crazy as it may seem, landlord, son, tenants, all alike, we all went out for a drink together. My dad was the governor; he got the money and we did the work in the place. There was not one tenant at that time who did not do some kind of job in the house if they got behind in the rent. My dad got us all working for him at one time or another. When I had to pay my way, I paid for my room – it was seven pounds a week in those days. My dad did not give anyone the easy way out; we all had to pay our way. So we kept that old house going the best we could.

One night Micky and I got up at three in the morning and put galvanised sheeting across the wet, windy roof. Later on we used felt, tar, old zinc, anything we could find to patch it up with. Everybody in the house gave a hand and did the best they could. We patched it up so much that you could not patch it up any more. Micky was getting into trouble with the cars, and the police were after him. Mag got so annoyed with Micky that she told him if he did not stop his hobby she would leave him. They pulled out of Fairholme and went up to Halifax in Yorkshire. They got a place up there for themselves and the kids, but it did not last long before they broke up. They came down to see us all from time to time.

We had an old boy who lived in Fairholme, just two doors down from us. His nickname was Taffy. He was a gambling man; he did not care what he did as long as he had money for the habit. He would turn a blind eye to anything for the horses. Taffy would let the young kids or anyone, use his place for sex, drugs, gambling or any racket, as long as he got some money out of it. I knew Taffy's son and wife; they left the place long before he got into his bad ways. They were good people and hated what he did as a sideline. He did go to work; it was a good cover for his type of business.

One day Mag came to see us; she looked in a bad state. She was looking for money. She came down from Halifax with a really nasty-looking guy with a scar down his right side of his face. I asked her how Micky was; she said she did not know as she had split from him some time ago. The complete story to happiness was gone when they left Fairholme. Yes, when they pulled out from there, their lives changed. Again Mag asked me for a few bob but I did not have much money on me at the time. I was always giving or lending out money but I never got it back. I used to give Patrick, Micky, and other blokes money. Sometimes they tried to give it back, then when one loan finished, another started. I did not mind, as those people to me were not just people who lived in the house, they were my friends. To some people they were rubbish as they did not even try to or want to understand them. My dad and I did; we thought a lot of them so we gave them a few bob to keep them going. At this time, Mag was desperate for money and I knew what she was going to do to get it if she did not get it the right way. She was making for Taffy's place, maybe to sell herself to get money for the kids and get herself back to Halifax. It was nothing to be ashamed of; a lot of women had to do it. I can understand those who would be ashamed to do it, yet I do not knock those who do have to. You don't think about being ashamed when you have two hungry kids to feed and keep; when your man is gone and you are hooked up with a guy who steals any money you have. I begged Mag not to go down to Taffy's place. She asked me if she could see my old man. I told her he was upstairs, tanked up, sleeping it off. My father would not turn anyone away.

We had another young girl who lived in 29 Fairholme. I will always remember the guy she lived with. He had a deformed foot. She was a lovely girl, dark hair, small, plump good-looking, with a baby face that had freckles. She looked so beautiful, a beauty from County Kerry. She looked so Irish. She and this guy had a baby boy after a year of living in our place. They split up; I never knew why. I only know that Brett Jones, who left a month before, was good friends with her guy. I watched this young beauty destroy herself in less than one year. She got hooked on crack and other drugs. In no time this beautiful girl was a full-blown junkie. She sold herself to keep her habit going. When she was in our place she was always outside the door with her baby and the other women and kids. Sometimes it got on my wick, seeing them all standing around. They seemed to be having a good time. I guess it was me. I was tired after a long day at work, and, as time went by, I got used to them being there. Little did I and they know that it was coming to an end for them. They had the security of 29 Fairholme. That was going now. The young Kerry girl found life too much. She was proud, never asked for money, not from me anyway. She got worse. The kid's life in general got too much. She could no longer cope. When I saw her down Fairholme Road, I said, "Hallo, how are you?" I could see from her eyes, which were popping out of her head, that she was getting bad, yet there was always a smile on her sad, baby face. She was now looking worn out; along with her worn, beautiful body, which now was a thin shell worn from misuse. I knew she was dying. I never saw her again. Some months later, a guy going down the street told me that one of Taffy's whores was brown bread, meaning dead. I hit this guy right in the face. Though it was nothing to do with him, it was the way he said it that upset me. It made me feel sick. I did not see Taffy but I did put his front window in. Taffy was used to that being done lots of times.

Just to go back to my two old friends who used to live in the basement, Dick and Mac – Dick got so old that he went into an old people's home. He came out and back to see us all, time after time. He loved the crack, with my dad and all in Fairholme. One day I met him coming out of West Kensington station. He was standing half up; his back was badly bent. He could not stand up straight. He suffered from asthma and used to fight to draw breath in and out of his lungs, puffing like an old steam train. You would never think it possible that this frail old man who went babbling on with one dirty, filthy mouth at the station, could have been in three armies in one lifetime. As we made our way to the pub, Dick wanted to know where my dad was. He said, "I told Danny I was coming down today. Where is he?"

I told him he had gone shopping up Northend Road. Dick replied, "Yeah, shopping in the fucking Seven Stars pub, more like it."

I said to him, "Never mind, you will see him later."

As we stood at the bar in The Three Kings, old Dick looked around and said, "Many's the good piss-up Danny, Mac and me had in here."

I asked him, "How did you get the name Dirty Dick?"

He said, "'Cause I was always swearing as a nipper."

I could well believe it too, as every word Dick said was dirty swearing.

Dick continued when I bought him a drink, "You know, not just a fucking few miles up the road from here, life all started for me." I looked into his tired, worn face; as he spoke his eyes lit up. He shouted out, "Yer Chelsea Barracks, I was just a bleeding kid, fourteen years old in the bleeding band, blowing a bugle. I took the King's shilling; it was nineteen fifteen. Four years of it, went to France, got hit in the chest, fucked up ever since then. My old man got me and run me off with him to Ireland, not to have a go against them, but for them. He was a mick. I landed up, with him in the Free State Army, me a bleeding Londoner! When the troubles broke out, he got the call, didn't he, and me, well, I had no call– he collared me along. I was not too bright in those days," he said, looking across the bar. By now he had a full house listening to his story. As he continued he said, "I went everywhere the old man went. I was shit-scared of him anyway. It was all over in twelve months. My old man left me, he met some old tart and shacked up with her. I never saw the old bastard again. I got the boat back to Holyhead and the tram down to London as fast as my two legs could go, mate."

I asked him, "What was it like in Ireland in those days?"

His face turned and looked sad. He said, "It was fucking hell. They were starving in the cities. We had loads of grub 'cause we was Free State government troops, chasing rebels all over the place. Civil war wasn't it? Worse kind of war; they were all mixed up. Hate broke out between themselves. The people were okay, good. Mind you, I felt sorry for them; they had hell from the Black and Tans, and our lot, the Free State soldiers before then. They were getting it again from their own, the IRA. Anyway it was all over when they killed the governor on our side – a bloke called Collins. When they did him, they put the cat amongst the bleeding pigeons. We were running like blue-arsed flies, looking for a bloke on their side called Dev. We did have a good laugh one day. There was this lot up in the forecourt buildings; they would not come down. We got a long-range gun sent over from Winston Churchill.

We got them down. Then it was a lovely city; we had blown it to hell, us and the British before us. Bleeding rubble everywhere. I was glad to get out of it. They say it's a lovely place now."

I asked him, "What did you do when you came home?"

He replied, "I settled down, met me missus and we had two kids. One night she done the dirty on me. Money was scarce in those days. I caught her one night with a sailor in our boozer. I found money in a bag under the bed. I did not ask her any questions; I only belted the fuck out of her. I killed her in the boozer lav. I tied the toilet chain around her fucking neck; she did not open her legs to anyone after that.

"I had to get out of the country fast. My mate and me left on a boat for France. He was wanted for armed robbery. The police had a good idea it was me that killed my old woman, yet I was told they could not prove it one hundred per cent as I left no fingerprints around. I wore rubber gloves from my job gutting meat in Smithfield Market. Here I was in Frog land, could not speak a word to anyone. We got down as far as we could to Southern France. In a small town we saw an ad board saying the Foreign Legion wanted men. We got a taxi, and showed him the address; he got us there. In we went and joined up. Ten years, no questions asked. I now wished they had hung me for my old woman's death. It was hell on earth – we got sent out to Chad. It was so hot, one hundred degrees each day. If you pissed up the wall, as soon as you had finished, it was dry. We chased the local wogs by day and had their women by night. It was nineteen thirty-nine when I got out. I was too old for the next one. I was forty years old, but I looked sixty. I came home. It was wartime. I got a ship from Spain.

"In nineteen forty, I had to stand trial for my wife's murder. I got ten years. On compassionate grounds, I got out in August nineteen fifty. I went from one part of London to another until I got to Danny's place. That was it," he said.

"Look at these kids in the pub. Going around with 'love, peace, make love not war' signs. Hippie power, that's what they call it," I said to him.

He replied, "Aren't they lucky? They have never seen killing, stinking dead or starving people."

One kid asked Dick, "Aren't you sad your mates are gone?"

"No, I am not. It is over for them. I have to live with it."

By now Dick was getting drunk.

"Give us a song, Pop," they shouted out. "Come on!"

"I will do better than that," said Dick. "I will give you three of them."

His eyes were glowing; the pub was packed. There was not a sound until Dick opened his mouth. Number one was 'We are the Soldiers of the Queen'.

"Me lads, up yours, me lads, put blue steel up the wogs' arses, me lads. We screwed their women by night, me lads."

That was Dick's vulgar version to the core.

Now for number two. He sang:

"Free Staters are we, have sworn Ireland to be free, we are a nation of a fighting race, that have never known disgrace."

Now for number three; "Soldiers of The Legion are we, in the French, in the French..." then he stopped; he had forgotten the words.

The kids shouted out, "Well done, old man."

The barman called out, "Time please, come on now, gentlemen. It's way past time."

I took old Dirty Dick down to the station.

"So long, Michael," he said. "I am sorry I missed Danny."

That was the last time I saw Dick. He did write a few days later saying that he was in a home where the old men were made happy by two young tarts offering their services to anyone who had money. "At least I will go happy," he said. In two weeks he was dead.

Mac was different from Dick. For a start he was six foot four inches tall in his bare feet. He had a size forty-eight inch chest. The son of a Durham coal miner, who came from Ireland, Mac was hard as nails. He had a love-hate relationship with people from down the south of England. He said they were too soft and had it easy compared with people up north. Mac came down south for some of the so-called easy life. I got talking to him one summer's night outside our house. It cost me four bottles of Bowman's cider to get him to open up about his life. As he continued to speak to me, he started to trust his secrets to me. After all, to him I was just a young kid, starting out on life's road. He knew his life was almost over.

"Well now, Michael," he said, "where was I?" He was thinking. "Oh yes, I came south, joined the bloody guards. Mind you," he pointed to me with his finger, "I won't tell, you what lot I was in. I will tell you this – I got to the rank of sergeant and a most trusted one. My colonel had all my background checked out before he trusted me. Well, the top brass never gave anything away. They took what they wanted and used us like toys. We were there to be used as a service. Bloody hell, I can tell you about the services."

Knocking back the bottle to the last drop of cider, Mac carried on talking.

"My colonel picked me out for diplomatic despatch duties – in other words a fucking errand hoy. The colonel was told by the MOD to keep an eye on the foreign diplomats in Kensington. He used six other ranks as well as me. It all looked like a cloak-and-dagger cocktail mixer to me; it was all a load of cobblers to give us something to do. I did not mind a bit, as it got me out into civilian life a lot. I got sick of kicking young kids up the arse that could not soldier, so one afternoon the colonel sent me around to his house to pick up his despatch letters. The house was in Kensington Mews. A young maid opened the door to me, looked up at me and said, 'Can I help you, sergeant?' I said, 'I have come to get the colonel's mail.'

"The maid said, 'Can you wait here, sir, I will tell milady.' Out came a tall, thin, good-looking woman, with ginger hair laid back on her head.

"She asked, 'Can I help you, Sergeant?'

"'Yes, mam, I have come for the colonel's despatches, ma'am.' She stared at me.

"'Come into the drawing room, Sergeant. That will be all. May.' She dismissed her maid. She quickly closed the drawing room door. 'My name is Monica, what's yours, Sergeant?'

" 'Mac MacCarthy, mam.'

" 'Oh dear,' replied Lady Monica, 'we don't have to be so formal. I like Mac best. You are new here, Sergeant. I have not seen you before.' She was now looking me up and down with her big brown eyes. I said, 'Aye, mam, this is my first despatch to the colonel's house, mam.'

" 'Well,' she smiled at me. 'Let's hope it's not your last, Sergeant.' She was putting me to the test. My eyes became lit lip and were wide open. In my mind I knew what her game was. I would not make a first move; too much was at stake on my side. She was now getting hot for me; she was mad for me. She kept looking at me, her eyes roving all over my body and uniform. Then she spoke. 'My, what a big lad you are, Sergeant Mac.' I did not open my mouth; she had said it all. I was amazed, too astonished for words. I was going to hear in my ears what she wanted; she turned around in a silly way and said, 'Listen to what I am going to say to you.'

"I stood still. 'Yes, ma'am. I am all ears,' I replied.

"Lady Monica gazed up into my face and said, 'I require your services. All the time you come here, Sergeant Mac. Do you get my meaning, mister. Do we understand each other?' There was a demand in her voice.

"I said, with a smile on my face, 'Oh yes, Lady Monica.'

I did my duty to the full. I do think that cow of a colonel's wife thought I was a bloody acrobatic performer because she wanted it every way – on the table, on the floor, up the side of the wall. She would have done it on the fucking ceiling if she could. I found out that all six blokes who called to the colonel's house to pick up despatches were despatching Lady Monica one. Every time they called she was mad for it. She was a fucking gymnast at it in that house, and she had the nerve to ask me if I had any venereal diseases when the bitch must have been full of it. One afternoon, after giving my services to the colonel's wife, I caught the young maid helping herself to Lady Monica's silver. She looked at me and said. 'It's only going in for a cleaning, sir.'

" 'Yeah,' I replied, 'to the pawn shop cleaners.' The maid got frightened; she dropped the silver on the floor. She got up as fast as she could, with some of the knives and forks in her hand. She had tears in her eyes. Bursting out crying, she said, 'Please, oh, please, sir, don't tell milady. I will do anything, only don't tell.' I knew I had her where I wanted her. She was frozen still. 'I will lose my job,' came the pitiful plea again.

"'No you won't' I said, 'if you do what I tell you.' And she did her services around the back at Kensington Gardens in the bandstand one summer's night."

As Mac was a strong, strapping lad, it was not just women who were after him in the army. There was some really hard-looking men who were homosexual and of high rank. Mac said, "These men were not soft in any way; if they fancied you, and you were not sexually attracted to them, then if you crossed them you paid for it in other ways. They gave you hell. I was not becoming anyone's nancy boy. One night I had a few drinks in our mess room and this big, queer bastard came up to me. I knew he was one of them. I never opened my mouth to him. He smiled at me and whispered in my earhole, 'I will have you tonight, Sarge, before the night is over.' I turned around so fast and kicked him right in the balls; as he started to fall down, I put my knee into his face and broke his jaw. I got court-martialled and drummed out of the Army with a dishonourable discharge. My army days were over. I went back up north, bought a boat and lived on it for a time. I had money saved from my army days."

Mac went back in time again. "I will never forget that old colonel's whore; she used to leave two half crowns on a plate when she was finished with you." Mac was bitter about her; you could see it on his face. "Fucking cow, she used us," he said. "I did not have any trouble finding a job when I got out," he said. "I have worked for mobs and hard men all over. I've done bouncers' jobs – that's the end of the line when you are a big bloke like me and you can handle yourself. It's a degrading job for anyone my size with a bit of a brain."

I asked Mac what he did with all the money he made. As he spoke, he looked at me and said, "Well, I pissed it up the wall with wine, woman and song."

I asked again, "All of it, Mac?"

He said, "Yes, why not – I look at it this way – I came into this world with nothing and I will leave the same way."

My last question for him was, "How did you meet Dirty Dick?" He laughed in amusement at my question.

"In The Old Oak pub," he replied. He got up, leaving the empty bottles all around him.

I called out to him, "He is dead. Dick's dead."

Mac looked back. "He is better off out of this shithole."

Tears came rolling down Mac's face. 'He should have gone years ago, silly old sod. He hated soap and water."

Mac did like old Dick. He shouted back to me, "He was not a bad old soldier; he had a bad time of it, well, fuck it, so did we all. I tell you something for nothing, son, your dad understands us. Those bastards out there never will."

He went up the street; the drink had no effect on him now, he was so used to it.

He got behind in the rent like the others before him. My dad gave him time to pay but it was no good – Mac was past paying any more. He just got out of hand. He went from one hostel to another. Then one day I saw a crowd of people looking and standing around a church seat. There he was, lying across the seat. Someone said, "Give us a hand." He had lain out all night in the freezing cold. Yes, it was Mac, as dead as can be, just a cider bottle for company. I could do no more for him: I left him to the crowd. I did cry as I moved away.

Going back to 29, Fairholme again. We had the white people coming and going. A lot pulled out for good. I never saw Mag again. Micky did come back a few times; he had done well for himself with a young lady who had a few bob. Then we had the start of the hippies. First we had a guy called Monk; he was a black sheep. His father had a big company up north. He had a young girl with him called Shirley. They took Micky and Mag's room in the basement. One day Shirley made a cake and put marijuana in it. I did not know of it as I never took drugs without a doctor's prescription. They gave me a piece of this cake over in the Barons Court pub one night. We were all laughing and I did not know why. I was laughing for the wrong reason as the joke was on me. They all knew about it before and they all had a good night on me.

Micky was there too but Monk was getting real bad with the drugs. One night in the same pub, he nearly got a right hammering from a load of jacks as Monk insulted one of them. It was a good job we could run fast and they were well pissed. We were running like hell because we were shit-scared. These guys were ex-soldiers, plus they knew how to fight a lot better than we did. After all, it was their living. Monk ran back to the house and got the starting handle from his old car. What good that may have been, I don't know. I did not stay around to find out. Monk and I just kept running and running down Northend Road. After a time the jocks gave up and we went back into the pub. A few days later, luckily for us, the guys had gone – bar one guy. His name was Big Angus, and he was big and he was powerful – well over six foot seven inches tall, wide as a barrel, strong as a bull. Luckily for us, he was in such a bad state on the night that he did not remember too much, though he did look us up and down, stood back, opened his mouth and said, "Don't I remember you lads from somewhere?"

I looked at Monk thinking to myself, if it comes to him, I am going to shit myself. I said, "No, I don't use this pub much. I go to The Elm; that's my pub."

He looked away and said nothing. We were lucky; someone up there was praying for us.

Monk was getting so bad on the drugs that he would take anything. He was five ten in height and had ginger hair – he looked like Noddy from the pop group, Slade. Many people thought he was his double. I went down to his room one night and found him taking every drug that he could lay hands on. He made a cocktail out of a load of tablets, put the lot into one glass, filled it up with alcohol, put it in his mouth and took the lot before I could stop him. He was a hospital case that night; he took an overdose time and time again. Luckily for us, he and Shirley pulled out and left. Monk was the nicest guy you could meet when he was not taking drugs. It was sad. I don't know what happened to him or to Shirley. She was a pretty girl and well educated. How she got mixed up with Monk, we will never know. Maybe it was love.

We had one gentleman who was completely different from the rest of the characters that we had living with us. He had a problem too, in a different way. It was not a money problem, which most of the other people had, or a drug, or alcohol problem. It was the opposite. This gentleman had a big hotel on the island of Guernsey and life just got too much for him; he wanted out. He had a very high class, respectable family and he himself was a professional man. I think in his early days he was an army man. When he arrived at 29, Fairholme he had a car. I remember the smart French vehicle that he drove. I do not recall the make or model, yet it stuck out like a sore thumb from the rest of Fairholme Road. This man took our ground floor front room. He wanted to pay my dad three months in advance with the rent money, but my dad would not have that – there was no need, a month was enough. This man got very distressed at times; you could see by his face that he was full of sorrow and that depression was setting in to his mind. He had got rid of his responsibilities when he came to us for a time. He wanted to fit in with the rest of the tenants in the house, and he did. They gave him no sympathy yet they did make him feel at home with them. He loved to join them in talking and listening to them and their hard-luck stories. He felt like one of them at times, as there was no tomorrow for them; they lived for today. He liked their way of life. The one thing he could not understand was that he had money and they did not. They liked him to buy them drink, take them out, buy them food, just spend his money on them. To them he was a gift from God; they could not believe their luck. He used to ask my dad to come down and chat to him. Sometimes he was lonely. My dad did try to tell him to stop spending and wasting his money on the tenants. He also advised him that he would bring trouble on himself if he kept on doing so. I went into his room one day when I got no answer as I was collecting the rent on my rounds. I got the key and in I went to see if he was okay. There was no one in the room. I looked on the floor and there it all was – passport, cheque books, vast sums of money and a lot of personal belongings. I think he just wanted to get away from everything. He needed help very badly. He was with us six months. I do think he believed we were getting on to him; we did not take any notice at first. When I say 'getting on to him', I think he may have thought we would inform the police about him because he was well out of the usual. Though we did not inform the police, one day he got up and went and left everything behind him but he was a real gent. Three months went by and we had to do something, as it was the law then that you could not move anyone's gear from your premises. My dad decided to try and contact his wife, as we had seen photos of the hotel with the address on them. We kept all his belongings in my room. We were sure his family must have been very concerned and worried about him. His wife came and she asked my dad if he had informed the police. He said, "Yes I had to when he did not return." She was grateful to us for keeping all his belongings. My dad gave her all that he left behind. She gave him a full receipt for all she had taken and we asked no questions: the lady was too upset. We had done all we could. All the guys in the house spent days and nights looking around for him – that was typical of the people in 29, Fairholme . His wife thanked us all; she wanted to leave money with my dad and all in 29, Fairholme but he would not have it. His last words to the lady were "It's okay, lady, I will look after this lot."

She said to us as she tried to hold back the tears. "I can see why my husband was happy here."

Then she left. We never found out what happened to the real gent. We believe he must have flipped in his mind. Yes, they came from all walks of life.

It was now 1970. I was no longer the silly kid. I had learnt a lot, yet I was going to learn a hell of a lot more in that coming year. We took one more Irish couple in, in the old gent's room. They came from the West of Ireland, a place called Sligo. She was small, tubby and okay. She worked in a fish shop up Northend Road. Her other half worked on the buildings when he could. He thought he was real smart. We had someone nicking the post; at first we did not know who it was and could not point the finger at anyone. We used to find the letters in the toilet, tucked behind the cistern. After a time most of the people in the house knew that it was this guy. He did not know it but they were watching him. How the hell they did it, I don't know. He did not have any idea that they were coming up to me with a full report. One day I did drop a hint – it stopped. But that was nothing to what was going to come. This was the time my father and I nearly copped it. Our one-time family lodging house was about to turn into a living hell.

One day, this guy walked in the door with a rucksack on his back. His name was Ernie. He was about five nine in height, had black curly hair, a round face and dark features. My dad had advertised the front basement room down Northend Road in a paper shop. Ernie was the first to see it. He said it was for him and his brother. As a rule my dad did not give out to men; he always let it to couples. The one thing that my dad had not done for a long time was change the beds around. He took out a double bed and replaced it with two singles: that was his first big mistake. Ernie came in and for the first couple of days he was really quiet and smooth. He was just getting the lay of the land, as they say – the calm before the storm. We did see his brother only one time in the first week, then he dropped out of the scene for a time. I found out after that Ernie was a gypsy from a Hungarian family, yet he spoke with a London voice, clever boy. But Ernie was into making money, and he made money out of 29, Fairholme Road. In a way, he taught us all a lesson. When Ernie came in he brought in the hippies. In the Sixties and the early part of the Seventies, there were good hippies and there were bad hippies, like in any crowd of people, but Ernie brought the worst into 29, Fairholme. They were junkies and they used the place tor twelve months. They gave all the rest of the house and my parents hell. No one got any sleep, day or night. 29, Fairholme Road, became a police station. They did not need a police station m Fulham or Hammersmith: 29, Fairholme was as good as any law shop. We had the police down every night of the week. My dad lost control. He tried to play it as cool as he could. Ernie bought young kids in; they took drugs, they pushed drugs, they used it for sex and they used it for anything that could make money. The police came in with tracker dogs that knew all about drugs. The cops pulled out walls, took up floors, pulled out fireplaces; in fact they pulled the whole fucking place to pieces. When the woman coppers arrived, they got all the hippie women up against the wall. With one announcement it was pants down, legs apart, on went the rubber gloves and the search was on for drugs. They screamed the place down. When the police finished their job for the night, we had to put up with the madness and loud, way-out music. So Ernie went mad and had a good time on us. He packed them in. They came from all over. The rent law at the time was on Ernie's side; the good old Labour Party had seen to that. The tenant had control. Yet all good times must come to an end, so in the end it was a combination of police, council, and my father getting a court order to shift Ernie. It took six months to do it, it cost my father a lot of money, and for twelve months Ernie did rule the basement. One night, he came up and took a knife to my father, and put it near his neck. I was not in at the time. My dad said, "If you do, you will do life. And they know where to come, son."

He put it away, told my dad. "You won't get me out so easy," then left. By this time I had had enough of it and I was near breaking point. No way was I as strong as my father. I think I did bottle it at the time – it was the first time that I had got scared of it all. I turned tail on my dad. It was the first time ever, the first time I ever let him down, but I do admit I did let him down. I was ashamed of what I had done. It will always be on my conscience for the rest of my life.

The people who we had still staying in the house, stayed on and stood by my dad. Oliver lived in the basement. A guy who had lived in Canada for some time, was a great help to my dad. That guy's name was Chris. He was getting on in life yet he and my dad had a go at a few of the hippies who got out of hand. Though all this craziness and madness went on twenty-four hours a day, everybody stuck it out. We had an Irish guy in the back basement room; he stood his ground, though my dad did give him money to get him to stay, because if Ernie got that room we would have lost the basement. Ernie caused so much damage: he put out lights, cut LEB main cables and smashed windows, doors etc. In the end, my father got him out with a conviction from the police. I went to Ireland for three months. When I came back, my dad had done all the business; he had stuck it out and got rid of Ernie. The police came down one Saturday night and they at last found drugs. In the back of the fireplace was a wall with a brick that came out. They got the drugs with Ernie's fingerprints all over – his first slip up. They could never pinpoint anything on Ernie. This time they had a field day and they nailed him, not for one count, but many. They waited for him to come up the road into 29, Fairholme then when he came out they nicked him.

He was out on bail when he came back to 29, Fairholme to pick up his belongings. I was just back from Ireland. I let him in. I played it nice and cool with him. He said to me, "Do you want me to do you favour? You were not bad; you did not give me any aggro. I can get a tin of petrol, get rid of this place for you."

I said, "No, thanks, Ernie, I like this place. As bad as it is, it is my future."

Ernie went and we learnt a hell of a lot. My father was never the same afterwards. For one thing, he was frightened, though he never said. We were all frightened because we all could have been so easily killed in that house then. We had the Hell's Angels in there too. We had one scene where a guy came in, stripped a motor bike right down from handlebar to a full tank of petrol in the house. He also had a sawn-off shotgun. My dad took him nice and cool, asked him to leave, nice and slowly. The guy got up and left. He was no trouble – and if he was, who in their right mind was going to say so? No way! Bikers, they called them – no they were not all bad guys, but if you crossed them, you came a cropper. We never crossed them, never upset them. They used the place, there was nothing we could do; we just had to wait till they were finished. We took it easy and we survived.

I cleaned up, painted and papered Ernie's old room, then a man called John came and took it. John was okay; he loved rock and roll fifties and sixties music. Well, we all did, and life settled down a bit. By this time I was getting fed up with the old house; all the people I knew had gone and I was getting older. I was thinking of doing one of two things. One was to leave 29, Fairholme. Two was to make a break for the States. I did not do number two, as I met a woman who was to be my wife in the company I was working for, and that was the end of that.

Now the story changes again with 29, Fairholme. There were a few funny things that happened. I am going to tell you about what happened before I left 29, Fairholme Road.

Chapter Six

Whores, Gays, Psychopaths, 1973 to 1979

The next guy who came to stay with us was Don. He came from Edinburgh. He had a good education and worked in the city of London in a stockbroker's office. He used to train the young in the markets – or, as he said, the rackets. My dad showed him the room. He liked what he saw; he was taken in by what the landlord had got into one small room. Don, as we came to know him, gave an intelligent account of what was in the room: table, chairs, wardrobe, cupboard, sink, dressing table, bed, cooker, fridge, bed, clothing etc. Well now, out came the sound of Don's Edinburgh accent. "A man could be a king in his own right with all this accommodation. I will take it, Mr Mahoney. Now, if you require references, that's no bother. I can get them."

Dano replied, "That will be fine." It was now that the fun began. He moved in with bagpipes, a passion for electric lights and Willo. Don was West London's first streaker. He turned into a right nutcase overnight. He would run down to the front room in a blanket, look to see if the street was clear, then off he went in his birthday suit, running in and out of doorways, shouting "Here comes Willo, Willo, here for the lasses, catch him if you can, for he's a canny man, is Willo."

Don had two things going for him. One was there was not a copper on the beat who could catch him, he was so fast on his feet. Number two, Willo was the largest prick in West Kensington. I did not believe that it was possible for a man to be so big! One night, a copper was standing outside our place. I knew him. He said to me, "Mick, if I see him, I will have him, tell him from me."

I replied in a joking manner, "You can have him!"

Next morning the front doorbell did not stop ringing. Three young tarts were queuing up to enquire about the whereabouts of Willo. One London tart said, "I would give anything for one hour with that Willo. Right now my old man could not satisfy our cat."

Then her mate behind said, "What you want, Jane, is a blinking donkey."

By now I was getting pissed off with them all. Before I could say any more, up came this bloke dressed up as a woman, with ten tons of make-up on his face and a handbag hanging around his arm. He said to me, "Excuse me, am I at the right address? I have an appointment with Willo."

Well, that was it, the joke was over. The tarts took the piss out of the nancy boy. One shouted out, "Get in the queue, dearie!"

I said, "I will tell you lot what I will do with you, if you don't move your arses from this door. You get my boot up you."

One tart said, "Yes please, that's the best offer I have had all blinking day."

I said, "Fuck off, you understand that," and closed the door.

The words I heard from them were, "Up yours."

Two days later, I went to have a word with Don. When I got up the stairs I could see one hell of a shining light coming out of Don's room. I knocked on the door, was just about to tell him what the police had told me, to inform him, when he cut me short with, "I have seen the light, light has come, the Lord is here." You bet he was! My head said 'fuse box' before Don plus Willo could burn the house down. We knew we had a real fruit and nut case on our hands. The next thing was how were we going to move him out? The police were after him yet they would have trouble in a court of law unless they caught him red-handed; so one night, we did just that. As we had no phone in the house, it was not easy, so me and Hammersmith Police waited for Don and his Willo to make a move. All night went by, then at five a.m. he made his big cock-up. I did not understand why he left it so late. He got six doors down Fairholme when he ran right into the arms of the law. So that was the end of Don and Willo! We kept his gear until he got out of Wandsworth nick.

It would take a lifetime to tell you all about the people who lived in 29, Fairholme in my thirty-five years of experience. No doubt I have missed a few out but the ones I have mentioned were the characters of 29, Fairholme Road.

For some more, I would like to go back to the time of Mr Cummings. Late in the afternoon, he and Dano came back from the pub. Dano got Cummings into a spare room in the ground floor. He tried to explain to Cummings that there were two doors that he could use to get out to the toilet. Dano put him in there so he could sleep it off. When Cummings woke up he did not have a clue where he was. He stood up, walked right over to the window, pulled it up and pissed straight down into the basement. The only trouble was there was a guy called Mick down there! He had just finished washing his hair after a day's work on the building site. It was a lovely summer's evening. Unfortunately for Mick, he got it washed again! This time it was a little bit stronger then shampoo. Mick went wild; he came flying up the stairs to sort Cummings out. He was a good six foot in height plus he could handle himself; he had been a bouncer in his time. By trade he was a first class plasterer, along with working for some hard men. Yet he was the nicest guy you could meet. He did me a few favours in pubs many times, when the odds were against me. Luckily for old Cummings, Dano heard all the noise. He got there just in time. My dad had a go at Cummings and stopped Mick from hitting him because if Mick did, he would have been in big trouble as old Jimmy Cummings was on the way out of this world. In less than one month he was dead from drink and drugs that he made up himself

Then we had one little old man upstairs who was a retired jockey. It's amusing how people get their kicks. He made a few bob, in other words, he made money. It is funny how some people pick the way they want to live. There was this old woman called Kitt. She was an old, worn out prostitute by trade. She was in the pub one night when she got involved with the jockey. He brought her back to the house. Dano knew Kitt by seeing her in the pub. Though he did turn a blind eye to the likes of her, if he caught her on the premises, he would have her out, or any whore. He was red-hot on that and so was my mother. The jockey had some weird ideas of what he wanted to do with old Kitt; after all he was paying her for her services. We were sitting down to have our tea, when we heard a load of shouting and racket coming from the jockey's room below. We heard Kitt shouting, "Dano, Dano!" My mother just done her nut when she heard Kitt's voice. It was like a red rag to a bull. My mother was down the stairs before we got up from the table. She was banging on the jockey's door demanding to know what was going on. By this time Kitt had kicked the jockey where it hurt, and got to the door. Our tenant, the jockey, had a tonic made up for his guest and that was a full bucket of stale urine that had been hanging around for days. He poured it all over this unfortunate broken-down prostitute. Old Kitt yelled out to all who could hear. She said, "In all my fifty years of being on the game, I have never experienced this." She stood on the landing dripping and stinking of piss. We could not get her out the house fast enough. She kept shouting, "I will have that bastard yet. You're dead." Poor old Kitt staggered up the road. In the meantime, the jockey locked the door from the inside and thought it was a good idea to set fire to himself, plus the whole house. Luckily for us, his room was soaking wet. After a visit from the fire brigade, ambulance and the police, they got together and broke the door down. They got hold of the jockey and took him away; his riding days were over.

In Fairholme, we cleaned the room, left windows open for a week or two, redecorated the room, took up the lino, creosoted the bugs and got it ready for the next case. The next guy was quiet – we could not believe our luck, or so we thought. We did not know that half of Europe was looking for him. To think of it now, it makes me quiver, sends a chill down my back. This shy, slim guy, five ten, dark hair, a bit like a Greek, who stayed in our house, was wanted by Interpol. He seemed okay, never said too much to anyone, paid his rent on time, was out all day and said he was working in a hotel up the West End.

Then one night, I never saw so many coppers in my life. They came from every direction. The whole Metropolitan police force must have been down Fairholme Road. They did not have to knock at our door; it was always open. They came in like a herd of cattle, no questions asked, just shoved a photo of this guy in my face, then knocked on all the doors in the house. Then a voice came out from this copper with so many pips on his uniform that all the coppers nearly shit themselves. If we had been all asleep, by now we were wide awake. My dad showed the top copper the room that this guy was in. Then the coppers rushed up the stairs. One of them said, "Stand back." Then out came the firearms. Two coppers stood each side of the door with guns at the ready. The police told everyone to get back in their rooms. The officer in charge asked the guy to come out with his hands up in the air and to walk out very slowly. I thought, "Oh, no, not again. We have only just repaired that door after the jockey." It did not happen. The shy, quiet man came out nice and calm. It all went real smooth. It was hard to take in that this gentle-looking guy was a cold-blooded killer and he was sleeping under our roof.

When we got to the ground floor, I asked a copper I knew, what the hell he was wanted for. He said, "It's worth more than my job to tell you that. You will read all about it in the West London paper in the morning." True, he was right. The police did not leave right away as they had questions to ask all the household. At last we got out in the street for some air. I looked around. I never saw so many law cars; the street was full of them. I did not hear a sound coming out of number 19; it was a well-known brothel for full-time activities, day and night. Like rats, all the tarts in number 19 had gone to ground. It was the first time in so many years that I had not seen a light in the joint. Taffy's place was also like a graveyard, no gambling going on, not one junkie or pusher to be seen. It was all quiet on Fairholme Road's Western front. The Old Bill had a clear-out all along the street.

We had one old boy whom my mother took in one night as she felt sorry for him. I don't know what made my old man agree to it. He was a nice old boy, getting on in life. It was not a lodging house he should have gone to; it was a hospital he needed, or a nursing home. For company, he had a little, yellow, singing bird. He was very ill and we could not find any living relation. So my mother looked after him and fed him. He had money. We did not know my mother was doing this on the quiet; the old boy was giving her money. When my dad found out, he put a stop to it. The old boy got so bad that we got on to a hospital. They sent nurses down two days a week. The old boy died within the week. My mother found him just two days later; the singing stopped in his room and then the bird died. It was sad that this old man came in off the street to die in a stranger's house. He was not with us long, yet he went in peace.

We had some nice people living there, like Jim and Anne. Jim was a great worker, fast; he did a lot around the house for my dad. He worked on the roads with the gas company, plus the building game. He had a way of saying, "Sound as a bell, boss,' when he did any work, and you could be sure it was done right. They were good friends to me in 29, Fairholme; in fact they were the last good friends that I came to know in Fairholme. We would go to the pubs and dance halls – I had a good time. Like all good things, it came to an end. Jim and Anne went home to Ireland to have a family and who could blame them? They saved their money as they both worked. I did miss them when they went.

It was not all bad, though we did have some funny, wild people, plus the best conmen; we had them all. I left in 1977; I got married. My dad kept my room for me because he thought the marriage would not last. This was the time the gay era hit Fairholme Road like a tidal wave. They came from Ireland and Scotland. I don't know what happened north of the border – in Glasgow it must have emptied overnight. West Kensington was full of Scots. Don't get me wrong – they are not all bad; there were good and bad, just like it was with straights. The Scots took over some of the pubs like The Three Kings, The

Old Oak and a few more. My dad did not even know what the word 'gay' meant, let alone think about homosexuals. He could not, for the life of himself, understand two men fucking each other, though he did not know he now had half a house full of them. When I told him this information, he replied, "What am I supposed to do, look up their arses when they come in the door?"

It was now 1980. I had left the house three years earlier. I had no idea what the old man was taking into the house. The first queer I saw in 29, Fairholme was a guy called Ray, back in 1969. He was really funny, and a great guy to have around. He played the piano down in the pub, The John Lilly. Ray was a great laugh; he always made you laugh when there was a funny time to be had. I must say, he never tried anything on with you if he knew that you were straight. One day, Dano did catch him with a guy in his bed – the guy took an overdose, to make matters worse, so out went Ray. He came from Yorkshire. I never saw him again, though he did come back and say he was sorry for causing trouble, and that 29, Fairholme was the best home that he stayed in in London. I wonder if he is still alive.

The first guy in the Eighties that Dano took in who was queer was an Irish guy from Dublin. He was okay. He worked on the buses. When Patrick left, he gave this guy his cat. A few years later, when my father died, he went to the priest and asked him if could say Mass for old Dano and the cat that died in 29, Fairholme Road. That guy thought more of that cat then he did of the human race. He did well – he got out of Fairholme and bought his own flat. I think he got embarrassed with the way he was in 29, Fairholme.

Next came Ian. He took my old room. Ian was not a bad guy. To Ian, my dad was the father that he never knew. He came from a family of fifteen kids; he had a Belfast mother and his father was Italian. Ian was born in Scotland. For a guy who was a homosexual, he had a family of two kids somewhere in one of the Scandinavian countries. It was very sad, in a way, with Ian. He was a fine-looking man but he had got so mixed up with the wrong type of people. I saw him as a good guy; he was not the type to harm anyone. He had a hard time, mostly because of what he was. I think no one has the right to hound or brand anyone because of what they are. Ian became very attached to my father. There was nothing sexual in it – Ian just loved the company of Dano. You would never think that Dano was Ian's landlord, or anyone's in that house, though when Dano was on the bottle, it was a different story. When he was sober, we all knew then that he was the boss. Ian liked Dano's way of carrying on and they became good drinking pals when my mother was not around. In other words, Ian liked the crack and chatting to Dano. The trouble with Ian at this time was that he let the drink take him over, as it can do to you when you start. Ian had a good job working for the parks department, yet he was frightened that he could land up getting into trouble by getting involved with the public. He stopped going to work; the drink got to him and he lost control. It was sad, as he was getting good money. His pals stopped coming to see him. I told him to stop drinking with Dano, as Dano was getting old. I tried to tell Ian that he was only in his forties and had his own life to lead – plus he would not be around if he did not climb out of the bottle. I said to him, "It is okay, and bad enough for my father to be drinking so much, but, Ian, he has lived his life; you have some way to go, don't waste it."

Things were changing fast in Fairholme Road; the prices of houses were going up. Fairholme Road was changing from hippie land to yuppie land. My dad had not done a hell of a lot of major repairs to the house but in the early part of the Eighties the local council came down on him like a ton of bricks.

Chapter Seven

Decay, 1987 to 1988

He had to put in a bathroom where there was no bathroom before and replace all the doors with fire doors. He had to spend money on the old place. One of my father's brothers had died and left money to the family. It was a big help to him and it paid towards the alterations that had to be done. He always thought he had modernised the place but the fact was in no way did he do that to the standards of today. He did what they required. He managed to survive and keep the rooms. At this time my mother got sick again. What started her off was that Ian started to bring in his friends who were homosexuals but they were not bad. They had a few drinks but there was no real aggro as such; they may have had late sessions of drinking, yet there was no real damage done. However, it upset my mum. She had a go at Ian and his mates. It got worse: she was now getting hold of the old man's drink. He could no longer cope with her; she was too hard to handle – plus the fact she was getting older. I had to come over from where I was living in South London at weekends and start giving care and attention to them both, because they were getting too old to care for themselves. My dad was a very proud man; he always had the dignity to keep himself clean. He had always looked after himself all his life. He did not want help from anybody; he always paid for what he got.

This part of 29, Fairholme is sad and tragic, as this was the beginning of the end for my mother and father, and the people who lived there. My father was coming up to his seventies, and in the eighties he barely managed to keep control of the old place. Some came in to the house and did things that they thought he did not know about, but he knew what was going on; he knew all the tricks they got up to but he just turned a blind eye to it all. He was getting into a bad state. One week they would pay him the rent, next day they would ask him for a loan; then they could not make it this week and so on. He kept some of them going. They were okay. If they could not pay him one week then they would pay him the next. As time went on he was now slowly losing control of the house, and he knew it. We had gambling men too. One guy was Joe; he did a lot of work around the house and he got me out of trouble before I left. Though I paid him, he told me when he first came to 29, Fairholme, that he got very sick and had to go into hospital; he could not pay Dano until he got on his feet again. That was okay by Dano; he kept Joe's room for him. But that was Dano – he was a hell of a generous man; he also knew a genuine person when he saw one. He was a good-natured man: no one ever had a bad word to say about him that I know of I am not just saying that because I was his son; all the people who knew him respected him. They did not have that same respect for me, but I admit that because I was a different man from my father, I was a bit ruthless in a way. But I have learnt a lot from him. As the years went by, he was always the cool character, he never took the bull by the horns and he never went into a china shop and smashed all the glass. I was young and did not have the experience that he had. I learnt the same ways as him.

Then came 1987 and my mother was in a very bad state. She was getting so bad that she was walking around the house naked. From alcohol and tablets, it was too much for her. I know she missed me not being around the place; I was the only comfort that she had. She felt safe when I was around. Now I was gone from the house; after all, I was her only son who she had to cling to. She was like a cat. My mother had nine lives; she was on death's doorstep so many times that I do not care to remember, but she survived. My dad was starting to drink really badly, like a fish, because he knew he was getting old. The thing that upset my dad too, was that I had no kids, and that there was no one to take over from me. Not that I wanted anyone to take that place. I would not want any child to go through what I went through. My father did not see it that way. By now my father was slowly giving up, but he would not give up until the end. He was on a bottle of whisky, a day now, from September 1987 to February 1988. I could not stop him drinking. He used to fight with me like hell; he used to tell my wife that I liked fighting with him. Maybe I did, in one way. I did respect him and I loved him, but my father was not a man to whom you could show love. He never cried in front of anybody, nor ever showed his emotions; only once did I ever see tears in his eyes. That was when his sister died. Some years before they did not get on too well; when he was younger. he told me, one time he upset her and she let him have every plate she had in the house. She smashed them all in temper. Yet she was family and her death upset him a lot. That day there were tears in his eyes. He could cope with anything brilliantly. A lot of men would have broken down; in no way could they have stood what he had to put up with: a sick wife tor twenty years, a son who disappointed him in lots of ways. Yet, the way he wanted to live, keeping that big house going, was not easy. My mother and I had no choice; she loved him – that was the way it was in those days. A woman would not put up with that kind of life today. Most would take off and who could blame them? She and I did not, because it was not just a home, it was all we knew. Now they had gone so far that I had to go over to take care of them every weekend. It got terrible, tragic. I took the blankets, sheets and their clothing over to the laundry. I washed and dried it all and cleaned up the place at weekends. I brought tins of soup and cooked them food. My wife cooked a chicken; I brought it over with me at weekends and left it for them to eat. We were fighting a losing battle all the time.

We tried to keep them alive a bit longer. I got worried about them; I did not know what I would find some weekends. Life is amazing: how people land up or wind up. I could do no more for them; in that respect I did not know myself I was always used to having to cater for myself when I was a kid; not many kids had to do what I had to do. I learnt to cook at ten years of age and look after myself, sew my own clothes and wash and iron shirts before I went to school. It was not a bad thing, though it is not the right thing for a child to have to do. A lot of kids had a great time at Christmas; it was not always so for me. My Christmases were sometimes very sad. There were times when I had to cook my own Christmas dinner or went without one. When I got older, I went to a friend's house who I have not mentioned so far. They were his uncle and aunt, but they were terrific people and I used to go and have my dinner at their place and they gave me a Christmas, an Irish Christmas. I used to dance; I loved the Irish music and the way of life they had. It was a break from Fairholme. I had never forgotten about Ireland. I went back a lot when I was younger in school holidays and my early working days. Ireland, was always in my thoughts. I upset a lot of people when I married my wife because she is English. I never thought I would marry a Englishwoman myself. But there you go. I was mad with the English for what they had done to the Irish in the past. I read history books and studied things when I got older. Sometimes I felt very dejected about the whole thing, and I took it very personally when I was very young. As I got older, I grew out of it and started to accept people for what they were.

My dad and mum were getting on now. I had to hold down a job; they could not cope any longer – plus the fact that 29, Fairholme was getting out of hand again. My dad knew it; though he would stay sober for three days of the week, four days of the week he was drunk out of his mind, though he always claimed he knew what he was doing. When he was younger he would do business just as well when he was tanked up. In those days he did know what he was doing, but now he was getting older and he did not. People were starting to take advantage of him in lots of ways. It is not fair for me to say that people robbed him. As such, I think he left the temptation there too much. They looked after him in that house. It is not for me to judge anyone. He left himself wide open sometimes, and money is a temptation to all of us. I was no different to them when I was living in that house. I admit, sometimes when I used to think he was half tanked up and asleep I used to go through his pockets. But I think he knew it and sometimes he would play at being asleep. He told me he always slept with one eye open and most times he kept his trousers under his pillow. He would turn a blind eye when I was a kid. He never in his lifetime laid a hand on me. He only had to look at me – that was enough; I was shit-scared of him. As far as fighting, I would not consider taking him on because he would knock me into the middle of next week. Even as an old man he had one hell of a hand. It's all very well people saying, don't rob an old man, but when you are desperate for money you will do anything. Dano used to give the tenants in the house money to go out and get him alcohol as he was desperate for it; it was now the only thing keeping him going, yet it was slowly killing him. It eats into each day; it was eating his brain and body. He did not care. He gave one of then a twenty pound note; the bottle of whisky probably cost seven or eight pounds. He got so much change back. He might say, 'keep the change' or, 'have a drink'. Sometimes when he got so had he got no change back, it did not worry him as long as he got the whisky. I remember just before he died, the early part of 1988, he accused me of robbing him, which I did not. He had ninety pounds missing out of his cupboard. The truth is, we never knew if he drank it or gave it away, or if it was stolen.

It was now December 1987. The hospital had had enough of my mother's complaining; also the day centres were a waste of time for her. She was gone beyond any help from them. She was getting no proper food, not enough vegetables; living on tea, fags, drink, tablets, bits of food; she was just skin and bone. The only thing Dano was cooking was bacon and eggs but in the end he could not even do that. They were getting meals on wheels and he used to eat hers when she could not eat it. It was sick to have to watch it happening to someone that you love. After all, they were my mum and dad. What could I do? It was just sick decay.

I went back in my mind to the time I was trying to get a place of our own. I asked my dad to lend me four hundred pounds, to help us get a place. It would have got us in the door at the time. He never lent me the money to do it. He said to me that this place was mine when he was gone; in other words, he wanted to hang on to me. He did not want me to marry; he thought I was too young to marry, though I was thirty years of age. He wanted to keep me in 29, Fairholme for life, just to keep the old place going. Why do fathers think that sons will look after them in their old age all the time. Some do, I can tell you; others won't. I did do the best I could but I know in my heart that I should have done more. I did want to live my own life. I was happy with my wife and the life we lived. I was out of Fairholme – that to me was a godsend, though I knew one day I would have to go back into that house again and it would eat me up too, as it did my father. I was now living in rented accommodation, along with my wife, in South London. I walked out of 29, Fairholme Road with money I had saved up and a wedding gift of an ironing board, plus the price of Fulham Town Hall for our wedding day. My father paid for the use of the hall for our wedding fling; my wife wanted a big wedding with all the trimmings. When I think about it today, I think it is ridiculous – it cost a thousand pounds then. But that's what she wanted. When I think about it now, it was stupid because we could have used that money to get our own home.

In the meantime, 29, Fairholme Road was getting out of hand; it was getting ridiculous, when I think of it. The door was open all night; the police were calling all the time trying to tell my dad to keep the front door closed. It was like an open house with guys bringing their so-called friends back late at night. The place was more like a public house than a lodging house. They came for a good time all the time. Like the song says, 'let the good times roll' – they never stopped in 29, Fairholme and my dad had got to a state where he did not give a monkey's. He was too far gone to care. He was advised by his accountant.to spend some money on the house, as it would help him with his tax bill, so he did the house up outside; it looked nice, but inside was a mess. The rooms wanted papering and painting. The hall had not been papered in ten years; I was the last one to do any work on it. The basement was sinking fast; the joist was giving away in places. There was dry rot in parts of the top landing. That should have been repaired some years ago. The roof was in a bad condition as it had had so much botching in thirty-five years. On top of all this, it was still a fine building. The house had taken a bashing.

In a way, it was a shame the way it was mistreated and abused over the years. To my father it was a business moneymaking proposition. That's all it was to him.

My mother, in the meantime, fell down the stairs, as my parents still lived on the top landing. She had to go into hospital again. This time she really did hurt herself – she fractured her hip. The hospital had to do a minor operation on her hip. She was lucky to be able to walk again, yet she did. But when she came out, the authorities had had enough; they told my father that my mother would have to go into an old people's home, so she would be looked after, get her food and be stopped from getting any alcohol whatsoever. He was upstairs and would not move down for anyone. We had to get him down on the ground floor as fast as we could. We did up the rooms on the ground floor. The welfare people came in before we had done any work on the rooms; they took one look and thought it was disgusting. One officer's words were, "It is a disgrace." Just before they walked out the door, we guaranteed them that the next time they came we would have the rooms redecorated, and we did, though my father did not want it done. You try and convince an old man who is dying and has had enough of this world to paper and paint a place! After a lot of moaning, he gave in and moved down. He had to have a load of whisky inside him. He felt sorry for himself; it hurt his pride. He knew it was the beginning of the end. He did not like being on the ground floor; he liked being on the top floor. He used to say to me, "Up here, I am away from them. It's the only bit of privacy I can get." When he could no longer climb the stairs in the way he could in the past, he knew it was getting too much for him, yet he did not want anyone to see the way he was getting. He now had a walking stick; he used it to get around with and, if you upset him, I am sure he would let you have it, so the stick came in handy.

Dano hated the thought of my mother going into the home. He fought it for three months, then I took him down to West London Hospital to see the doctors and welfare authorities. They told my father it was the only option now left: he alone had to agree to sign the papers to confine my mother, his wife for over forty years, to a home in South Croydon. It killed him; he got so worried about her. He said to us, "I am bloody glad she's out of here, not upsetting the house anymore." That was just talk. Now he missed her and he pined for her, though when she was there he could not get a word out of her. Yet he was glad; she was company for him. He used to say to me, "You're leaving that woman here to die. Get her into some hospital." They were married forty-two years – that is a lifetime twice over in my book today.

I said to my wife, "I now realise the situation in my mind. It comes to the hard fact that I may be able to save one of them, but I cannot save both of them." My dad told me the only way I would get him out of that house would be in a wooden box: well, that was not strictly true but not far off it. The next thing he found out was he was going to have to pay for her fees in the home and they would take the income out of his house and he would have nothing left out of it. That was the final straw, and the final nail in his coffin. I could not stop him drinking and he just drank himself to the end. I contacted his brothers in Ireland. We had the phone installed six months before he died and I got them to phone him; they talked to him and he listened. There was nothing they could do. He never believed in having a phone in the house.

I now come to a sad and tragic part of 29, Fairholme Road in my life, when I saw my father cold sober for the last time. One night I went around to empty the electric meters in the house. When I arrived he told me, "There is no need for you to do that job, I have already done it." That was Dano, proud to the end, his own man, his own boss. He offered me a fiver for coming over. I have my pride too – I refused to take the fiver. He turned around to me and said, "How many houses have you got?'"

I said, "None," and that was it. It was sad in some ways; he never wanted me to leave but I had to go and I left.

The next time I went around was after receiving a phone call from Joe to say that he had fallen out of bed and was in a bad state. He had cut his head and had been lying on the floor for some time. We called a doctor out and after some time a female doctor arrived. She examined him and said there was nothing she could do, only to put something cold or frozen on his head. She sent me up to the shop like a schoolboy to fetch a frozen packet of peas. She said to take away the drink and to try and get him off the drink. I told her the only way was to get him into a drying out centre. She said for him to go in he would have to be cold sober. Sometimes I think it was the most stupid and foolish system that the health authorities ever came up with. How do you try and save a man's life when he has been drinking non-stop for over a full year? I think sometimes the people in these authorities have not experienced enough of people like my father. My dad told me that if you take a man off drink right away you can kill him. He said he once saw that happen in Dublin. There, with more experience, they just wean them off the alcohol bit by bit. It took time. I may have been able to prolong his life a bit longer, I do not know, if the doctor could have got him in somewhere at an early date. My wife did try so hard. She went over one day. The doctor said he had to be in there by nine a.m. My wife got over just after nine a.m., around nine twenty. Dano was ready to go; my wife phoned the doctor when she got to 29, Fairholme. The doctor said it was too late. Well, when I heard that I felt like going over to Fulham and kicking that doctor right where it hurts. It hurt me more but I know now that two wrongs do not make a right. What do they say? 'Don't buck the system?' My dad was going fast. I could not stop him. He had no will to live. His wife was in an old people's home. It was all getting too much for him now.

Three weeks before he got bad he was not shaven. We went up Northend Road for the last time together. We went in the bank and he paid a bill for his taxes. He paid all his outstanding bills before he left this world. He left with a clear bill, not owing anything to anyone. He had the bill for the old people's home to pay as well. He was not too happy about paying, yet he did pay it. I brought him down the road. He looked very bad – he had lost so much weight, his face was drawn in. He looked like death warmed up. He was a fine, strong-looking man, now gone to waste from drink. I took him into a cafe to get him something to eat – he loved bacon and eggs.

It was sad the way my dad went: if you saw him, he looked like a tramp or a dosser. He had not shaven for weeks. He smelt of sweat and drink. I walked down Northend Road. People looked at him. I felt so bad I walked in front of him; I did not have the guts to walk beside him. He must have felt like Christ did when the world sent him to his death. I know that now. God forgive me, I felt so ashamed of him then. Now I feel guilty, more ashamed of myself for not standing by his side – after all, he was my dad. I did get him into one little barber shop that always shaved him and cut his hair. He always gave them a good tip. Dano had a great laugh on him, was proud and thought nothing of what people thought about him. He loved the crack and would talk to anyone. He would help you if he could.

He now looked a bit better. I took him up to see my mother at the old people's home. This was a tragedy in one way. It was the last time my mother saw him alive. She was so glad to see him she cried, "Dano what am I doing in here?"

With tears in his eyes, he said, "Well, Dolly," that was my mother's nickname; he said to her, "I've done all I can."

There were no more words, only two old people like young kids holding hands. He kissed her with an old man's mouth, yet the kiss was like a young man's passion. For me it was good to see them together again, my mum and dad. I was lucky to just have them there for that short time. Some kids, sons or daughters, never get to see that scene in a lifetime. He was half sober. As he had a silver plate in his head, he used to shout a lot. They got a bit worried in the home as he had a bit of a go at this old boy who would not move away from where my mum was sitting, so Dano gave him a mouthful in a nice way. He had that sort of way where people would turn around and look at him. He would attract attention very easily, more so when he had a few drinks in him, but he was harmless, never troublesome. He was always smiling, laughing at what people had told him – maybe it was a silly joke. He was some character. Someone told me he would have made a great actor.

When he left the home he was looking for a pub. I brought him around the long way, away from the sight or smell of a pub. Little did I know that in two weeks' time he was going to have left this world. It was the worst thing I did, in some ways, yet he was not fit to go into a pub. I think now I was right; I just wanted to get him home safe and sound. As we made our way back to Victoria Station, he turned round to me and he said, "There is no need for you to go any further. I know my way back from here."

So I said okay to him. I asked him, "Do you want me to come back with you?"

He replied, "No. I have got to see the dinner lady, to make sure she has left the dinner inside the door for me."

That's all he thought about, getting his bit of grub, in the end. I felt guilty. I felt that I had done him wrong. I felt I should have taken him home on the train. I should have stayed with him but Dano was not that type of a man. Like I said before, he was his own boss. He did not want you feeling sorry for him. He wanted no one's pity. He used to say to me, "I got on in London before I met you. I know the way to go." Even though he was half tanked up, he knew the underground system like the back of his hand. Before the war, long before I was born, he was using the underground. It was the last time I would see him walk. He looked bad; his back was bent as he struggled to walk to the train. I always saw him, in the past, standing with shoulders back and arms swinging, eyes in front. He was never in the forces, yet he had the best discipline in him from his younger days. He wanted to join the navy in the war. His eyes let him down; though he never wore glasses he had bad eyes. A bad car accident in the war put paid to that. He had a military mind; it was a waste and a disappointment in his life. We all get them.

The following Monday night I went around from work to see how he was. He was in a bad state now. I told him. "You must go to hospital now." He tried to say it was a waste of time. I phoned for an ambulance right away. It took them half an hour to come.

The ambulance driver said to me, "How many more in the house have you got like this?"

I said, "Never mind about them: I am only concerned about him." I got my dad into the ambulance. We went to Charing Cross Hospital in Fulham Palace Road. I took him in and sat there from seven p.m. till nine p.m. before anyone even stopped to take a look at him. I had to go around and nearly get on my hands and knees and shout. "For fuck's sake, will some arsehole of a doctor take one look at my father?" This was our good old NHS system, working at its best. Is this what my father and I paid out money for, to keep this madhouse running? Yes. I saw people worse off than my father. I saw guys with broken heads, arms, legs, blood all over the place, old, sick people hanging around waiting for someone to pop up out from nowhere. I guess they just had a bad night and my old man just happened to pick the wrong time. A doctor did see him and he was lucky to get a bed for the night. He had cut his leg and it was now in a state where it had festered. A nurse had called to 29, Fairholme Road. I don't know what happened; it looked as if she could not get into the house as the door was closed, at last. That house had the door open on a latch twenty-four hours a day and the time she was to call, it was closed. Well, I find it so hard to believe. Some people in the house say my father gave the day nurse a key to the front door. We will never know. The people in the house did look after him; to the end, they thought the world of him because they knew that, when he was gone, their world in 29, Fairholme Road was going to change too. Their cheap way of living in Fairholme Road would also be gone, so everybody tried to keep Dano going for as long as they could. In some ways I was thankful to them for that, because they did try and do the best for him, but Dano was beyond any help in the end. Before I left the hospital, they told me my father was dehydrated. They looked after him. In a way, I was relieved. I knew now he was safe in hospital. He was not alone in a bed in one room, with a bottle of whisky under his pillow, both sides of him and nothing else – plus the fact that the only heat he had was from the old type electric fire. The room had the appearance of Charles Dickens' times, only they did not have electric fires in that time; the rest was Victorian – unbelievable for this day and age. Dano loved all the old in anything he got. He used to say to me, "The old is best; it lasts longer then the new rubbish that's out today." How right he was. He was a man who loved the past and its style.

The next day I went back to work. That Tuesday night I went to see him; he did not look too bad. All he was on about was his keys and his money and how the house was and who was looking after the place. I told him I was staying for a while and he seemed to be happy with that. I returned to work for the rest of the week and went to the hospital again on Thursday night. Again, Dano looked okay and was getting ready for the road back to Fairholme.

Meanwhile, on Friday morning at my work, I got a tightening in my chest, then a full belt of pain. Was it coincidence? I did not say anything to anyone. Was it just a pain? I had left a note with the hospital ward where I could be contacted in an emergency. I gave them my work's phone number and my home number. I don't know what happened; they must have lost the paper, or what I said had gone in one ear and out the other. They were certainly not organised that day. I went back to 29, Fairholme that evening just by chance, I don't know what for. I was going to go home but something made me go back to the house. I guess I was trying to keep an eye on the place. The one thing I did tell my father when I visited him in the hospital was, "Don't worry if anything happens to you, I will be straight in that door, I will be back there." I think that relieved him a lot. He was glad of that, though he did not say if he believed me. I don't know. I had told so many fibs in the past. I think he knew I was telling the truth this time. On Friday at around twelve-thirty, my father had a heart attack, unknown to me. How I found out was that I got a message saying, 'Contact hospital straight away'. As I picked up the note from my father's front room door, I knew in my heart what I feared most had now happened. A policeman had called in the daytime. I had got a priest to him before this had happened, some weeks before. The first person I saw in the house was Tom. As Tom could not read or write, he said the policeman left the note and a young priest had called to the house early on in the day. Poor old Tom; he was so upset. Ian was the next person I saw. He came up to the hospital with me and I was glad of his company.

When I got to the hospital I found my father lying in a coma. As I looked at him fighting for breath, the clergyman came in and smiled at me. "It's okay, son, he's had all the business." And there was no more we could do. At this time a lot of things were going through my mind – one was how I was going to tell my mother. I hoped and I prayed, believed he would survive the night, and he did. I left the hospital that evening; around nine p.m. the priest told me to go home, that there was no point in hanging around the hospital. I went back to Fairholme Road where I spent the night.

After phoning the hospital on Saturday morning and being told there was no change, I made my way back home from West Kensington to Thornton Heath, which is a fair old run on public transport. I had just had something to eat when the phone went: it was the hospital. The nurse said, "If you want to talk to your father again, you had better get back here quickly, because he has just come to." My wife came with me. We got over as quickly as we could to the hospital. He was now in the intensive care unit. Outside there was a protest going on; the nurses were protesting over cuts and pay rises. I looked over at them. When I got into the room I said, "You had a heart attack. You have been in a coma all night."

He looked over at me and said, "Glad you are here. I am finished and life goes on." That was the last words he ever said to me.

I went to see him on Sunday and Monday. On Tuesday the doctors told me he had no will to live; he was not helping himself or them. They had done all they could. They told me, "If he makes it past Friday, he could well pull through. It takes anything from one day to ten days to get over it." He was not responding to any treatment. Each day I went in to see him, he looked as if he was enjoying the company at the nurses: he was trying to laugh. I think they took a liking to him as he had that big smile on his face. By now he could no longer talk. There was an Irish nurse there – she did like him a lot: I could see that in her eyes. She had a sad feeling for Dano, though she never said so.

Only when she propped him up in the bed, she would say, "Come on, Dano, you can do better than that. Sit up now, that's a good lad." It sounded funny – he was three times her age. Yet she meant well. The nurses did believe he would pull through. I had listened to what the doctors said. That evening I went back to 29, Fairholme Road, alone. I sat down in the front room, the biggest room in the whole house. I cried alone, then Ian came down from his room. He asked me how Dano was, I think Ian was more upset than I was; he showed more emotion than I did. I was too numb to show any emotion; it was there but I was too numb. I was too worried and concerned about my mother and the house. In my mind, all the things he had taught me were buzzing around in my mind. I had been to his solicitor three weeks before he really got bad. I felt alone, even though I had my wife, who was a great help. But I felt alone in Fairholme Road, for the first time in my life. I had never felt that feeling before. Even though I was there, down through the years, people were there. There was always someone to go and talk to. This time I did not know anyone there who I could really talk to; they knew my father but I did not know them. Except for Oliver and a couple of other people, all the old crowd that I knew were gone. These were one hundred per cent my father's tenants. They knew him. They were not the same as I had known before.

On Friday, the phone went at ten to seven. A nurse with a Cork accent said. "I am sorry. Mr O'Mahony, your father's gone. He passed away this morning."

I was so tired and weary from going backwards and forwards to West Kensington and Thornton Heath. The nurse said she did try to phone me earlier on. I was tired; I must have slept through the phone ringing. I could not get the right time of morning that he died; I was not particularly worried. He was gone. That was enough. My world had collapsed. I was frightened, really frightened. I felt so alone. Dano was never frightened of anything, only the one time, when he had the trouble back in seventy-one, though he kept that bottled up. He told my mother many years later.

I now had to go through the rigmarole that everybody has to go through when you get a death in the family. My wife helped. I got in contact with his brothers, who came over from Ireland. We arranged the funeral. My father asked me some time back that when he did die, to make sure all the tenants in the house were asked to go to his funeral. I did that. Out of ten of them, nine of them went. I went to the old people's home and told the matron that I was coming to tell my mother the bad news. She was the last one to know. She looked so happy before I broke the news to her. She knew he was in hospital. I had told her that much a week before, though I did not say how bad he was. With a smile on her face, she asked me how daddy was. I looked at her; she read my mind as my face changed. How, in God's name, was I going to open my mouth? At first, the words would not come out from me, or was it that I would not believe he was dead? I said to her, holding her, "He's gone. He had a heart attack on Friday." It was now Sunday.

She pulled away from me and just bawled out, crying, "Oh no, Dano, Dano!" It cut me in two. When it was over, they gave her something to make her sleep. On Wednesday morning, my wife went to the home and brought my mother home for the funeral. My mother started to ask my wife, Maureen, questions all way back. Like how much the coffin cost, how much was the funeral, and so on. Maureen had a job to handle her as I had to go and meet my father's brothers. Maureen took her to the Chapel of Rest in Fulham. My mother walked in and stood by the coffin. I was not there. She was seventy-six years of age. She just wet the floor as she looked at my father's remains. It just came from her; shock had hit her, her world was shattered. Her man was gone, her home was gone, she was in an old people's home. It had all come into her mind. When she was in the old people's home, she did not know where she was, it happened so fast. She asked where she was going; she never knew the place or the area she was living in. I had to do some terrible things m my life; a lot of people have to – some people escape a hell of a lot of things by getting others to do it for them. I buried my father in North Cheam. It was his wish, as he and my mum could not agree, though we were all born in Ireland, to go back to the one spot, so we stuck to London. My father bought a plot there and that's where I put him.

I came back to 29, Fairholme Road. I had to go and see my father's solicitor. A game was starting that I knew nothing about; I had no experience whatsoever of dealing with death duties, probate, inheritance, capital gains, taxes, that, within the next twelve months, came down on me like a ton of bricks. I did not know what to do with the house; I did not know whether to keep it or sell it. I had a hell of a lot of memories there. It was a big house with ten rooms, not counting bathrooms and toilets. There were ten tenants in the house – four I knew very well but six I did not know well at all. I had one guy who was going to give me a lot of trouble but in some ways I don't blame him. My solicitor advised me badly at the time. I know that now. I was going to take his room and make it our bedroom. I got a builder in to give me quotes on the roof, basement etc., the whole house. It would have cost around one hundred thousand pounds to put the place right and into flats. I did not have that kind of money, though I could have got it from the bank. In return they wanted the deeds of the house and I would be up to my eyes in debt with them. After thinking it over, I knew what I had to do. I also had my mother to think about; the DHSS knew she had an interest in the house. My father's will was as follows: if I kept the house, she was to stay in the rooms that he occupied at the time of his death for life, rent free; also she was entitled to half the money that came out of the house; if I sold the house, she was to have half the use of the money that was left in trust for me, so I had to invest her half. I could not do what I wanted to do with the money until she was dead, then it would all come to me. I could do what I liked with my half, that was the way my father tied me and my mother up, as he knew she could not handle money. Luckily for me, the deeds were in his name only, as my mother was not in her right frame of mind. I had to go to the courts to get the legal rights to act on her behalf. It all took time. Probate took six months because of the boom in the property market. Houses were selling like hot cakes, solicitors were having a field day and estate agents were bringing clients like lambs to the slaughter. Everyone was making money fast. The banks could not give the money away fast enough. It was the time our Maggie said everyone should have his own home, no matter what the price. We all paid for that one later. I made up my mind that I had to sell it. In a way, it broke my heart. My father, God rest his soul, would have turned in his grave if he knew. "Never sell it," was what he said. I had no choice. The rents his tenants paid were a joke for that area.

Chapter Eight

My Last Days of Fairholme, 1989

We had one lovely old character there. His name was Tom. Tom could not read or write but in no way was he silly. He had a few bob saved, more than I could say for the rest of them, and good luck to him. He worked hard for it: his day started at four in the morning. He thought the world of my dad too. He came down to me one night and said, "Your dad died a lonely man, Michael."

I said, "I know. Tom." There were tears in Tom's eyes when I told him what I was going to have to do. I said, 'I am sorry, Tom. I have to sell it. There was too much wrong with it." I told him I could have got the money from the bank but it would have taken me my whole life to pay it back. I had to keep my mother in a home and that had to be paid for too. By now, the DHSS were breathing down my back because they thought she was the owner. They got that wrong. She did have a part income as I told them. I did not have to put the house on the market. There was a Pakistani gentleman, who had bought up half the street, unknown to me, back in the old days of a family called the Blacks. I am not talking about black people. They lived in 39, Fairholme that old house had a bit of a bad history to it.

When people think of Fairholme Road, they think of a bomb factory. Yes, there was trouble down there. A couple at guys got in there belonging to the IRA, or so it was rumoured. We all knew a policeman was killed, not far from Fairholme Road, by these guys. It was a nasty business. It did our street no good and gave it a bad name, but that was not Fairholme Road's fault. That could have been any road in London. It hurt the good people who lived in our street a lot. We all had to live with that hanging over our heads. But the Blacks' house was where this guy first started out, who bought my house. It was now my house, my late father's house. He bought number 39, Fairholme for seven thousand. It was in a very bad state but he did it up and let it out and never looked back. He bought more houses in Fulham and West London and I heard he had a few in Brighton. He had at least four in Fairholme Road.

For me, the worst part was I had to get everybody out, and that was heart-breaking. Like I said, one guy gave me trouble. He did damage to the house, broke pipes, and filled up a sink full of water and left it running. Part of the ceiling fell down and just missed my wife. She was out of the room for just a minute or so; if she had been in the room, she would have got the fallen plaster on her head. I had to replace the piping and repair the ceiling. I had to clear out all the house, and clean it. I did. It cost me three thousand pounds to get everyone into court. As I sat on top of the stairs. I felt really sad, because now it was the beginning of the end, for me in 29, Fairholme. My wife and I worked hard to clear all the rooms out. The antique furniture that my father had bought years ago was in a bad state now from cigarette burns and alcohol spilt over it.

Some of the tenants started to move out. Ian was the first. He was drinking a lot and had lost his job. He was getting behind in the rent; all his money went on alcohol. Ian got a little uptight with me – he had a few drinks in him – yet I know he did not mean it. He came down to say he was sorry, and he had had enough and was leaving. I gave him forty-five pounds. It was more than he had paid my father for a deposit for his room. I got Ian to sign an agreement to say he gave up the room and had his deposit. He said he was going back to Scotland but he went to Brighton. It is quite a place for homosexuals, I hear; that's not for me to knock or judge. Ian took off, leaving his passport and his belongings behind. I knew he would be back. He was and I gave him all his gear, with the understanding that there was no return to 29, Fairholme. I then got two more rooms empty. They were easy as the tenants were not there long.

Then that was it. I had to wait until October until I got the rest into court. I did it all legally by the law of the land. One day I went down to the courts with five of the tenants – John,

Oliver, Tom, Joe and Mahmood. It upset me. It seemed strange for a landlord to be talking like this. Yes, it got me down. It was the first time since my father died. I got very sensitive about the whole thing. One part of me was saying, "don't go through with it, Michael." Oh, how I wish my dad was still around, it was getting too much for me now. Could I go on? I had to.

I listened to all five give their reasons why they could not find a place. As my father lived on the premises, the law stood that I could have vacant possession within twenty-eight days. When the judge decided just that, I told my barrister to ask the judge, as it was coming up to Christmas, if he would give the tenants a few weeks longer. You should have seen the judge's face and the court room. No one could understand me, let alone my own barrister. I did not want to see these people, who were my father's good tenants, in bed and breakfast over Christmas. The judge smiled and said, "It's up to you, Mr O'Mahony. They can go, if you agree, from January onwards. How about January the fifteenth?" The barrister looked over at me.

I said, "Fine," to him.

The judge said, "All done." The court rose. It was partly over.

I had one more tenant to go; he was the guy who gave me the trouble. It was the other way round with him. I could not get him out fast enough, yet he got himself out in the end. It started when the judge gave him twenty-eight days too, only he told me in the court room I was dead. Well, I did not take that too kindly. I informed the police and they took it from there. He also started slagging me and my wife off. I took him nice and cool as I had more to lose; I had a house worth three hundred thousand pounds, to lose; he had only his arse to lose, so I put up with his drunken, dirty mouth for six months, and his drinking pals. I kept away from them all. He came down one night and started giving us a load of sick talk. I got the police and they had a word with him. It was a waste of time. He then played right into my hands by doing the damage he did. The police nicked him. The police asked me what the best time was to get hold of this guy. I said, "Well, if he's not pissed up, at seven in the morning; that's your best time."

So in they came. He did not know what had hit him. They questioned him there, and when they got him down to the police station, the policeman who nicked him told me he had admitted to saying he would kill me. Well, he was charged then and there, and told to get his gear out of 29, Fairholme Road. I got my room at the cost of five hundred pounds, the back rent I never got from this guy, plus the two hundred pounds I had to pay for the repairs that had to be done. I had to go to court one more time with him. This time I let him off the hook, as I knew that the most he would get was maybe three months inside. Then, when he was inside, his mates would smash in my windows, maybe set fire to the house, as he was behind bars. No, I told the policeman not to nick him, to forget it, that I was getting out anyway. I did not have to go to court any more. I let bygones be bygones. He was told to keep the peace for one year.

As far as I was concerned, he was the last bad guy we had in 29, Fairholme. My dad told me he was always behind in the rent. I thought that was a joke – he only paid twelve pounds a week and he could not pay that, living in the heart of West Kensington. He had a big front room on the first floor. At the time, my dad was soft with him. He took the piss out of him, and I knew it, and he knew that I knew it. He did not like me; the feeling was mutual. I had a go at my dad when he took him in. I knew he was a piss-taker.

Out of the six people, I did four of them a favour. They got council flats as they were in the over sixty age group. The others, no. I did not do them a favour. They lost out because they were younger, and the fact that they only paid a low rent in West Kensington did not help them. They paid around twelve pounds a week when most of the landlords were charging sixty pounds a room. It was a boom time in the housing game, buying or letting. My dad did not want to charge more because he had his pension. He knew he would only have to pay more tax and he did not want to rock the system. I did not blame him; the more you make, the more you pay in taxes. He was happy with what he had. He had a regular income coming in.

Christmas came to us all for the last time in 29, Fairholme. It felt empty. The house, and the tenants missed the laughter of Dano. It was the time of year when he gave a gift of a drink or a smoke or a small gift of some kind to all the tenants. He always did it as far back as I can recall. I did it for the last time. By now we only had four tenants left as Tom had moved out into bed and breakfast. I did not ask him to go; he just up and went. He came back to see us all at Christmas. I gave Tom, a bottle of whisky and we had a few drinks in the house with the remaining people who lived there. Tom came round a few times more before we left; as far as I was concerned, he was welcome any time. We liked old Tom.

My insides were sick with all that had happened in that one year. I was disheartened and so upset with what had happened. The place did not seem or sound the same without my mum and dad or some of the old tenants, like Patrick, Micky and many others. It was over; so were my days in Fairholme now numbered. As I walked down the street on Boxing Day, all the memories came flowing back. I knew every doorstep, each house, the kids that lived in those houses, each and every coal cellar. In my mind, as walked, I could hear the girls who lived in our street, singing and playing with a skipping rope, one at each end across the street. They sang this song: 'Along came Charlie, a fine, young man, he kissed young Jan, he cuddled her, kissed her, he sat her on his knee and said, will you marry me, yes, no.' And the kid in the middle had to skip faster until she was caught out. Happy days – not many cars parked in the street. The last big fight I had was with a kid called Tony. Tony beat the shit out of me many times but I still came back for more. It was the end of my childhood days. I loved that street and the kids I lived with. As I stopped at the top of the road, I wondered where they were now. I knew one was in Australia, my old mate John. Peter was in Canada.

My mind went back in time for the last time down Fairholme. My kingdom was going; the street I loved as a boy had changed. It was now full of cars and filth. Everywhere, the street was a mess and smelt of rubbish. There were black bags that cats and dogs had busted open and beds kicked out of houses. It was now a shit hole. West Kensington had now gone from A to Z, as far as I was concerned. I loved that place. I wondered where all my mates were now. The business of selling the house was going through; the guy I was selling it to could not get in the door fast enough to make money Out of the old house. God, if I had my way, I would never have sold the old place – I would have blown it up, but I had to be practical at all times. If I were not sensible now, my wife and my mother would suffer and so would I.

Christmas went and New Year came. By mid-January the bailiffs had arrived at 29, Fairholme. By law, they had to come. Before any of the tenants could get their new homes, the bailiffs had to make sure they were off the premises. That was the system. Everybody left. I then let our dog out to look after the house by day, as we were both working. I had a German Shepherd. She was not too friendly with people she did not know.

I do believe Oliver thought I would never sell 29, Fairholme. He had lived there some twenty-two years. I changed the lock on the front door and Oliver got a shock when he heard the dog running around the house. My wife said she was sure he tried to re-enter the house with his old front door key. I did let him back into the house as he had still more to pick up and take with him to his new address. He had already got something like ten boxes plus fifteen tea chests, all out of one room, and that was nothing to what I was going to fall over when I did get into his room. His room was the worst one in the house. It took us a week to clear it out. It was like a hardware store. He had everything from a nail to tins of petrol. We were sitting on a bonfire. I do believe our Oliver had gone out of his head.

Oliver was a genius with exceptional skill and electrical experience. He had a good head for doing things exquisitely. If it was not done right, Oliver would start all over again. If it was out one fraction, he would do it again. As the years went by, our Oliver got so used to my father buying everything he asked for. When he did even the smallest job, he kept it all in his room. It mounted up in twenty-two years. I found a building store in his room. Now I do believe that when someone says there is a hair's breadth between genius and madness, they are so right. I gave Oliver all the taxi driver could take. His back wheels were now caught up with his from, he was so loaded up. We said goodbye to Oliver for the last time and away he went. I don't know where he went to; he did not say. I do know he was a very sick man. He had heart trouble and the best thing was for him to get out of Fairholme, as he was sick. I hope he got a dry and warm place to live. Oliver was not bad; he was part of our family in 29, Fairholme. He was like a school kid. He would come and tell you everything that was going on in the street and in the house. I told him. "Well, my old friend, there is no more to tell about Fairholme. I'm sure you miss it all now." It was the end of an era.

As I said goodbye to Oliver, I went upstairs alone to the top of the house. I went in and looked around at my dad's old room, where his bed used to be, and the old furniture that filled the space of the whole room. I heard sounds of laughter in my mind and the voices of anger when he used to tell me off for doing wrong. Yet three of us lived in that room, plus two or three tenants on that small landing. As a kid, that landing was mine. It was like a ship's mast to me. As I looked down on the winding stairs and landings below, to me they were like a ship's decks: my ship's button was where I hung my flag on top of the landing with a broom handle; a child's imagination. Now I was taking my family's colours and flag down for the last time, in my mind.

I walked around the house for the last time. Every room had a face and tale to tell. I saw them all as the tears ran down my face. I heard voices shouting, "Michael!" Someone was outside Fairholme, shouting out up at the window. "Coming out tonight, Micky? Come on, Mick, we are going." We sure were. My wife had packed all for our new home.

I walked down Fairholme Road for the last time, that evening. Before we left the next morning, nothing came to me anymore; it was all gone. How I loved and hated that street! I just felt numb, like the day I laid my father down to rest.

On the twenty-fourth of April, 1989, exactly thirteen months from the time when I had returned to the house, 29, Fairholme was sold for the first time since the day my father put his foot in the door. That was thirty-five years ago. The business was done. The Pakistani gentleman had got my late father's and my house. My rule was over. I pulled out, funnily enough, in one of Nash's vans, that all the tenants had used, only the council paid for their moving. I had to pay for my own and rightly so. With me, I was not so lucky. Nash's staff had a bad weekend and I paid for it, as one guy did not turn up for work. He was a Chelsea supporter and he must have got pissed up or beaten up. Anyway, I had to help load up my own gear, with the help of two more gents, and unload it when I got to my new abode. In the meantime, my wife had become sick on the train going over to our new address. I left her to hand in the keys to 29, Fairholme with our solicitor. When she had done that, she had to bring the dog and a few bags and herself home on the train. She got sick on the train; I think it was all just too much for her and for both of us. It was all over. My Fairholme Road days had come to the end.

There are a lot of people I have not mentioned. I cannot think of all the names of those who lived there. You cannot cram every one into one lifetime. But they will know and so will all who lived there. They will remember Dano, Dolly and Michael and 29, Fairholme Road.

My story is over. Make what you like of it. I will never forget it for as long as I live.

Number 29 Fairholme Road. This photo was taken in 1973. Printed with the kind consent of Hammersmith and Fulham archives.